Tools for Promoting Active, In-Depth Learning

Second Edition

Harvey F. Silver
Richard W. Strong
Matthew J. Perini

Various lessons and ideas contributed by:
Judy Commander
Claudia Geocaris
Eva Benevento
Hilarie Davis

A publication of The Thoughtful Education Press

Design

Cheri L. Funke

Cover

David Efaw

© 2001 Thoughtful Education Press, LLC

227 First Street

Ho-Ho-Kus, NJ 07423

(800) 962-4432

www.thoughtfuled.com

Printed in the United States of America

First printing January 2001

ISBN 1-58284-004-0

Tools for Promoting Active, In-Depth Learning

Second Edition

(c) 2001, The Thoughtful Education Press
(800) 962-4432

(c) 2001, The Thoughtful Education Press
(800) 962-4432

Introduction: The Value of Tools

As educators in the age of standards, we constantly hear calls for more effective teaching and learning practices. We are expected to increase student motivation to learn as we guide students through essential content knowledge and develop the skills they will need for success in the 21st Century. Yet too often it seems as if these calls are coming from too many voices, hiding too many agendas, demanding too many contrary reforms. All of this makes the work of teachers more difficult than ever.

We call the techniques in this book tools because, in its most basic sense, a tool is anything that makes a job easier and work more effective. As teachers, one of the most important jobs facing us is ensuring that our classrooms are places where students are learning meaningful content, are motivated, and are developing the skills they will need for future academic and vocational success. If we are to create classrooms where all students can succeed, then we will need to have a variety of techniques in our teaching toolbox.

This book contains over 100 classroom-tested tools, or simple teaching "moves" that teachers can use to foster active, in-depth learning. These tools are based on principles of effective learning and brain-based instruction and require little or no planning. As such, the tools can serve as "on-the-fly" techniques whenever a learning episode begins to lag or new information needs to be processed, or they can be planned into a lesson or unit ahead of time in order to meet specific objectives. In either case, whether used spontaneously or as part of a pre-designed lesson, these tools will help students build essential learning skills such as:

- tapping into and using prior knowledge to learn new content;
- improving notemaking, vocabulary, and writing skills;
- developing memory, review, and practice skills;
- using questions and reflection techniques to deepen learning;
- developing meaningful products and performances;
- working cooperatively.

What is Active Learning?

Perhaps the most basic premise upon which active learning rests is that there are many more ways to learn than by being told or by reading a textbook. Learning isn't about having information poured into our heads; learning requires thought. As Confucius noted, "Learning without thought is perilous." Twenty-five hundred years ago, Confucius understood that learning is an active process. Much more recently, with current knowledge about how our brains learn best, many educators across the globe have worked to create "constructivist" classrooms. In a constructivist classroom, teachers ask open-ended questions and use student responses to help guide students through active learning processes like discussion, elaboration, inquiry, and metaphorical expression (Brooks and Brooks, 1993).

(c) 2001, The Thoughtful Education Press
(800) 962-4432

The common wisdom shared by Confucius and constructivists is this: In order to learn something well, students need to hear it, see it, ask questions about it, and discuss it with others. Above all, students need to "do it." They need to figure things out by themselves, generate their own examples, trust their own hypotheses, demonstrate their own skills, assess their own competencies, determine the qualities of their efforts, apply what they have learned to new situations, and teach others what they have learned.

Active learning, then, means more than engaging students in activities; it is a cyclical process in which participants constantly move between periods of action and periods of reflection. We learn by doing, but we learn more deeply when we take the time to look back, to reflect upon our actions, and to extract meaning from the data. The cycle then repeats itself again and again as we deepen and broaden our perspective.

Active learning is like a coil that constantly expands inward and outward. In that process, three actions are present:

Doing is the process of performing tasks that require some type of mental activity;

Looking is the process of becoming an observer of your own thinking and actions; and

Learning is the process of revising and synthesizing learning into a meaningful whole.

The following graphic representation depicts the cyclical process of doing, looking, and learning:

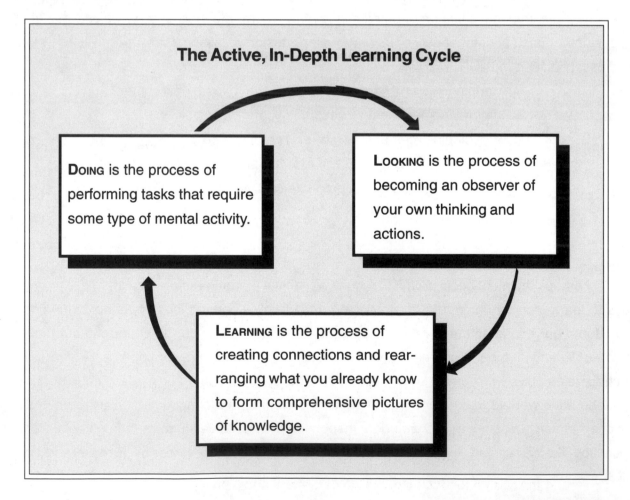

The Active, In-Depth Learning Cycle

DOING is the process of performing tasks that require some type of mental activity.

LOOKING is the process of becoming an observer of your own thinking and actions.

LEARNING is the process of creating connections and rearranging what you already know to form comprehensive pictures of knowledge.

What is In-Depth Learning?

Recent brain research (Caine and Caine, 1994) tells us that our brains produce two distinct types of meaning. The first type, called surface meaning, is similar to a definition we would find in a dictionary: a quick and general point of reference. While essential in helping us to develop a large storehouse of knowledge, surface meaning is neither comprehensive nor particularly engaging. It is a glimpse, a starting point, an invitation to look beneath the surface. The other type of meaning made by our brains is called deeply felt or deep meaning. Unlike surface meaning, deep meaning is rich and personally relevant because it has been constructed by our brains--actively processed; explored for its novelty and patterns; linked to experiences, feelings, or ideas; and situated within a relevant context. Because it is self-constructed, deep meaning is pleasurable to the human brain; it creates that same sense of satisfaction we get when we stand back and admire something we've built or when we have pieced together all the clues in a murder mystery to accurately predict who committed the crime.

To better understand the difference between surface meaning and deep meaning, think of the Statue of Liberty. At the surface level, the Statue of Liberty is a 151-foot statue made of steel and copper that was erected on Ellis Island, New York in 1886. From the perspective of deep meaning, the Statue of Liberty is more than just an object: It is a symbol of national heritage and the ideals of freedom and democracy. Many of us connect it with the goosebumps we got on our necks when we first saw it, or to the stories of our grandparents' hopes and struggles told to us at the dinner table, or to the idea of making a better life while also enduring a more difficult one in a new and strange country. In terms of deep meaning, the Statue of Liberty is not measured in feet or meters, but rather by the power of the emotions and the symbolic value we attribute to it.

The same distinction holds true for almost everything we teach. If we plow through a textbook description of the Civil War, we will certainly scratch at the surfaces of several dozen topics. But little of this information will be relevant or long-lasting for students. Students will never "own" this information. Most likely, they will remember it for a time--probably until the test--and then forget it. The situation will be very different if we orchestrate learning so that students connect the concept of civil war to their prior knowledge about how and why relationships break apart; develop visual depictions of essential concepts like abolition, sectionalism, and popular sovereignty; explore the mystery of why the seeming mismatch of the Civil War lasted four years in cooperative inquiry teams; create visual organizers like timelines and compare and contrast organizers to condense and summarize key information; and work in Writer's Clubs to draft and revise historical thesis essays on whether the Civil War was inevitable. In a classroom like this one, student learning is made deep in three ways:

1. *Students are building a permanent base of essential content knowledge.* A quick survey of the activities will show that instruction is focused on helping students construct a meaningful understanding of the central topics and concepts, the enduring ideas that are at the heart of Civil War studies.

2. *Students are motivated to learn and to do their best work.* All brain research tells us that the search for deep meaning is a constant and pleasurable activity for the human brain.

Giving students multiple opportunities and avenues to explore topics and demonstrate understanding (e.g., visual representations, inquiry, visual organizers, essays, discussion, Writer's Clubs) is a powerful way of motivating learners and energizing the classroom.

8. *Students are developing essential learning skills.* Education can no longer be exclusively about content knowledge. A large body of research investigating the links between education and contemporary careers (Resnick, 1987, Reich, 1992, Murnane and Levy, 1996) indicates that the new world we live in requires students to develop the skills of real-world problem solvers. In addition, new state tests and standards have also placed a premium on skills like interpreting multiple documents, analyzing visual information, summarizing, and developing evidence-based arguments. The emphasis placed on skills in this Civil War Unit (e.g., conducting an inquiry, developing visual representations and organizers, summarizing information, working cooperatively, drafting and revising, developing a thesis) means that students are not only learning how to succeed in and out of school, but also how to grow as learners.

We have written this book to provide you with specific, practical tools that you can use in all subject areas and at all levels to enliven your teaching and enrich your students' learning experiences. Using these tools and teaching students how to use them on their own will help you transform your classroom into a place where active, in-depth learning is the norm. But just as important, these tools will make the difficult work of teaching students easier and more effective. We hope that you find these tools useful and rewarding as you engage in the process of inspiring students to become active, in-depth learners.

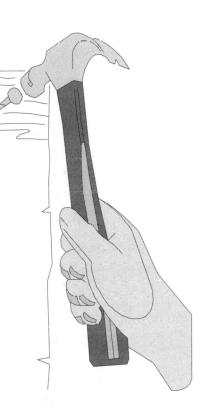

Tools for Generating Ideas

Think, Pair, and Share

Purpose: A simple technique for getting students to think and communicate cooperatively in a short amount of time.

Procedure: The teacher poses a question for students to consider. The students generate responses and share them with their neighbors in pairs. The teacher then collects the students' ideas.

STEPS:

1.   The teacher poses a question.

2.   Students think and construct a response.

3.   Students share their ideas with a neighbor.

4.   The teacher records students' ideas.

Example: *Based on our demonstration, think about how the boiling of liquids is different from the freezing of liquids. Discuss your ideas with your neighbor and be ready to share.*

Give One, Get One

Purpose: A technique used to initiate physical movement, to promote divergent thinking, and to generate many ideas quickly.

Procedure: The teacher poses a question and asks the students to record two responses. Students stand up and move around the room to make connections with other students. Every time a student "connects" with a new student, he or she needs to give the student a different idea and get another idea in return (new ideas should be added to student's original list). If both participants have the same ideas, they need to work together to generate a new idea. They then can continue their journey, connecting with other students. The teacher provides the students with a goal for the number of different ideas to collect and a time limit within which they have to collect them. It is important that students are reminded to work with only one student at a time (before they move to another student). Students should *not* form small groups to collect ideas. The point of the strategy is for students to meet other students and to move from one person to another, sharing and revising ideas.

STEPS:

1. The teacher poses a question.

2. Students generate two ideas.

3. The teacher establishes a goal (number of ideas) and time limit (time to collect ideas).

4. Students stand up and "connect" with one other student to give an idea and get a new idea. (If both students have similar ideas, they brainstorm together to generate a new idea.)

5. Students return to their seats when they have met the goal for number of ideas. (They can share ideas in small groups and try to generate two or three additional ideas.)

6. The teacher collects and records ideas to be explored.

Example: *How is a leaf like a factory? Generate two (2) ideas. Move around the room, sharing ideas until you have given and collected six (6) additional ideas in two minutes.*

Divergent Thinking

Purpose: A tool to help students think creatively, divergently, and originally.

Procedure. Divergent Thinking involves visualizing, or creating multidimensional pictures in the mind; imagining, or seeing possible relationships, causes, and effects; and using metaphoric language to describe and symbolize relationships. Divergent Thinking encourages students to explore ideas; list possibilities; improve or change something; expand or extend; place information in new contexts; re-group information; rename; invent; suspend disbelief; and suspend criticism or evaluation until ideas have been generated. It is used when you want students to generate many possible ideas or responses to the same question/problem.

STEPS:

1. Teacher poses an open-ended task, question, or problem: "How many possible ways..."

2. Students try to stretch mentally by going beyond their basic ideas.

3. Teacher establishes criteria for creative thought:
   - Fluency=number of ideas
   - Flexibility=number of different categories generated (EARTH and MARS would be two answers, but one category)
   - Originality=number of unique ideas

4. Teacher uses intuitive feedback to extend student ideas: "That's a possibility..."; "Who has another idea?;"; "What if we used this?"

Example: *Here is a sheet with twenty-five circles on it. You have three minutes to generate as many ideas as you can about what each circle represents to you. Write one idea in each circle. Remember to think fluently, flexibly, and originally.*

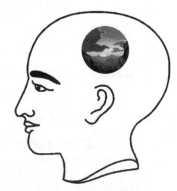

Use the following question stems when you want your students to exercise:

Fluency (creating as many ideas as possible)

- How many different ways can you . . . ?
- What words or ideas come to mind when . . . ?
- How is a_____ like a _____?
- What words/ideas come to your mind when I say . . . ?
- Think of an object--any object. What new associations come to mind for the ideas or object you've been thinking about (e.g., new uses of a pencil when associated with music, space travel, a house, etc.)?

Elaboration (developing more ideas from current ideas)

- Based on what you've written, what other ideas come to mind?
- If you think of _____ like an object, what other associations come to mind?
- When grouping your ideas, what new groups come to mind when you think of time, location, purpose, the material from which things are made, the forms in which ideas come, etc.?

Flexibility (breaking ideas down into non-overlapping groups)

- Group these _____by similarities.
- What new items can be added to the original or the relabeled groups?
- Using different metaphors, expand the content of your groups (e.g., How is a river like a book? A rose like a shoe? The west like the east? The sun like a man? The moon like a woman? A pond like consciousness? etc.).

Originality (thinking of things/groups unique to this activity)

- Provide a different ending for . . .
- Provide a different beginning for . . .
- Combine the following unrelated words into a meaningful sentence.
- Given a purpose and adequate data, design a plan to accomplish this purpose.
- Prepare a map using the following geographical data.
- Combine the following lines, shapes, etc., into a meaningful pattern.
- Design a symbol for . . .
- Create an icon that signifies . . .
- Given the following metaphor, create a poetic image for . . .
- Combine the characters from three different stories and write your own story.

Factstorming

Purpose: A technique used to generate as many facts as possible related to a topic.

Procedure: The students are organized into small groups. The teacher poses a question (e.g., How many natural resources can you name?). The students select a recorder for the group and generate as many responses as they can in a designated period of time.

STEPS:

1. The teacher organizes students into groups of 3 to 5.

2. The teacher reviews the rules for Factstorming.

3. Each group selects a recorder (or two).

4. The teacher asks a multiple-response question with many possible correct answers.

5. Students generate as many facts as they can.

Examples:

List all that you know about World War II.

How many geometric shapes can you name?

List the names of the parts of the cell.

How many parts of the body can you name in Spanish?

Brainstorming

Purpose: A technique used to rapidly generate multiple responses to a problem situation.

Procedure: The teacher organizes students into groups of three to five and selects one student from each group to be the "recorder." The class reviews the following rules for brainstorming:

1. *Inspect the question.*
2. *Develop as many ideas as possible as quickly as you can.*
3. *Stretch your thinking. Each idea should be new and different (think creatively and divergently), but you can build off of others' ideas.*
4. *All responses are acceptable. Do not respond to judge someone's ideas.*
5. *Work within the time limit.*

The teacher then presents a question or problem, and the recorder solicits one idea from each participant before proceeding to the next participant. Students are encouraged to build off of other students' ideas. The goal is to generate as many ideas as possible within the time limit. Once time is up, the ideas are examined for their quality. The group decides which ideas are **great ideas**, which are **good ideas**, and which are **just okay**. It is important to use all three categories. The students reflect on the criteria they used to distinguish which idea belongs in which group. Finally, students select the idea that they feel best addresses or solves the problem situation.

STEPS:

1. The teacher organizes students into groups of 3 to 5.

2. The teacher reviews the rules for Brainstorming.

3. Each group selects a recorder.

4. The teacher poses the question or problem and sets a time limit.

5. The recorder records each idea as stated (ideas should not be evaluated or critiqued). One idea must come from each participant before proceeding to the next.

6. Students are encouraged to build on others' ideas and generate as many responses as possible within the time allotted.

(c) 2001, The Thoughtful Education Press
(800) 962-4432

7.   Ideas are examined and grouped according to their quality. Criteria for selection are determined, and the best idea for solving the problem is selected.

Example: *What if the major rivers (Mississippi, Missouri) flowed west to east instead of north to south? How would it have affected the development of our country? Brainstorm as many ideas as possible.*

Graffiti

Purpose: A technique used to generate many ideas, to engage different styles of thinking, and to stimulate physical movement.

Procedure: The teacher generates sixteen to twenty questions covering a particular content area. Each question is written on a large piece of paper and posted around the room. Each question represents one of the four types of thinking: remembering, reasoning, creating, or relating. When generating questions, the teacher should also consider varying the questions according to the use of multiple intelligences (bodily/kinesthetic, verbal, logical/mathematical, musical, spatial, interpersonal, intrapersonal, and naturalist). Students are given markers and allowed twenty minutes to roam around the room and record a response to each of the questions. As they respond to the questions, students should think about which types of questions they enjoy answering and which they find difficult to answer. Students may also be asked to identify which style of thinking they believe each question represents. After students have had an opportunity to respond to each question, the teacher assigns a group of students or a spokesperson to study the responses and to summarize them with the class.

STEPS:

1. The teacher generates 16 to 20 question stems about a topic.

2. The questions should reflect four styles of thinking: remembering, reasoning, relating, and creating.

3. The questions can also reflect multiple intelligence perspectives.

4. Students roam around the room, responding to each question.

5. The teacher assigns students to summarize responses and report back to the class.

How are amphibians (frogs, salamanders, toads) similar to reptiles (snakes, lizards, turtles)? In what ways are they different?

***

How is the diversity of living organisms on earth like a treasure chest?

***

If you could be another living thing besides a human, what would you be? Why?

***

What plants are important in your holiday celebrations? Name the holiday, the plant, and its importance.

***

Can you think of a fairy tale that you like that has a plant or animal as a central part of the plot? Name the fairy tale and the plant or animal.

***

If plants could talk and move, how would our world be different?

***

Can you think of the names of ten different mammals? List them. Try not to repeat ones that other teams have already given.

***

Imagine a species of animal that lived its entire life cycle in an American classroom. What would its habits or special features be? Name it and draw a simple picture of it.

***

Examine the animals in the picture. Explain how these animals are adapted for living in trees.

***

Are dinosaurs more like reptiles or birds? Give at least two reasons for your answer.

***

What evidence do you have to support or refute the following statement: In their attempts to manipulate their world for their own comforts, humans have destroyed what they sought to control.

***

Do you think viruses are alive? Why or why not?

Carousel Brainstorming

Purpose: A questioning technique used to generate many ideas in response to different styles of questions, to promote group work, and to allow for physical movement.

Procedure: The teacher generates five or six divergent thinking questions that require more than one response (e.g., How is the atmosphere like a blanket?). Each question is written on a large piece of paper, leaving plenty of room for student responses. Paper can either be posted around the room or placed at different tables. The students are then put into small groups (3 to 5 students per group). Each group is given a different color of magic marker. Each group moves to one of the papers and begins to generate responses to the question. One student can record the group's responses. After two or three minutes, the teacher asks the students to finish and instructs the students to move to the next question. Students should first read the previous responses, then use their time to generate and record new ideas or to expand on existing ideas. Students should be encouraged to think quickly and to change recorders at each station. Once the groups have rotated all the way back to their original station, they summarize all the ideas written down at their station. An alternative possibility is for students to walk around the gallery individually and reflect on the generated ideas.

STEPS:

1. The teacher generates questions for students to answer.

2. Students divide into small groups. Each group uses a different color marker to record ideas.

3. Each group is positioned at each station for 2 to 3 minutes, during which time students generate and record responses.

4. When the time ends, groups rotate to the next question (or the question rotates to the group). Students read the new question, read the previous responses, and either develop new ideas or expand on existing ideas as quickly as possible.

5. The teacher asks groups to summarize the responses when they arrive back to their original station, or encourages students to walk around the gallery to read and reflect on the ideas.

Example: *Carousel Brainstorming Stations for a Unit on Natural Resources*

Chart for Station One (Metaphor)

Select one. Give three reasons why.
How is a natural resource like a video store?
How is a natural resource like a roller coaster?

Chart for Station Two (Visualizing)

Icons are visual symbols which represent ideas. For example, a picture of a skull and crossbones represents a poisonous substance. Identify three natural resources and create two icons for each.

Continued on the next page

Chart for Station Three (Classifying)

Group and Label: Examine the following list. Place the items in groups and label each group. Use your grouping and labeling to develop a classification system which will explain different categories and natural resources.

air	sunshine	waterfalls
sand	oil	whales
humans	trees	gas
iron	ore	flowers
river	tuna	copper
beavers	deer	buffalo
aluminum	kaolin	lakes
nickel	shrimp	rain
snow	magnesium	oysters

Chart for Station Four (Prioritizing)
Priority Pyramid

Determine the importance to man of the six natural resources listed by placing each in the priority pyramid from most important on top to least important on the bottom. Explain your reasons.

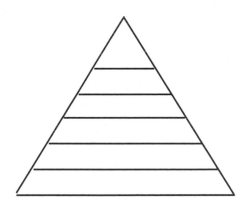

Resources to Prioritize: Diamonds, oil, soil, sun, water, wild animals

Chart for Station Five (Creativity)

Write a cinquain poem for one natural resource. The form is as follows:

Noun:	Coal
Two adjectives:	Black and shiny
Three action verbs:	Smouldering, burning, polluting
Four-word sentence or phrase:	A source of energy
Noun:	Factory

Tools for Activating Prior Knowledge

Context Connections

Purpose: A tool used to spark student interest prior to learning or reading, to help students make connections with various contexts, and to develop written explanations.

Process: The teacher selects a text, poem, article, essay, or chapter in a book for students to read (or to be read aloud). The teacher introduces the title of the piece to the students and has them generate their initial associations. Next, students write for 3 to 5 minutes on their organizer about what they believe the text is about. The students then read the text twice, once to acquire the overall meaning, the second time to reflect upon its meaning by using the following categories or contexts:

Self-based contexts

What personal experiences can I bring to this text?

Social & community-based contexts

How might it relate to the classroom, the school, the community?

Literature-based contexts

What have I read that relates to this?

History-based contexts

Are there any patterns that have been repeated in history or in the world at large that relate to this ?

Students discuss their reflections in small groups using the four contexts to guide their discussion. Each student then writes an explanation of the piece.

STEPS:

1. The teacher selects a text.

2. The teacher introduces the title to students.

3. Students write for 3 - 5 minutes on their organizer about what they believe the text is about.

4. Students read text twice: once for the gist; once for reflection in the following categories:

   - Self-based contexts
   - Literature-based contexts
   - Social and community-based contexts
   - History-based contexts

5. Students share their reflections in small groups.

6. Each student writes an explanation or interpretation of the text.

Context Connections Organizer

Title:_____

Associations:

I believe the text is about . . .

Contextual Connections

Self	Society and Community
Literature	**History**

Explanation of the Piece

Associations

Purpose: A technique used to spark student interest in a reading, to generate associations, to build an interpretation, and to deepen understanding of a text through dialog and writing. The tool works best with short pieces that have a central main idea.

Process: The teacher selects a short reading, poem, essay, article, or chapter in a text and prepares a triangle concept map for students to organize, collect, and develop their ideas. The teacher or students read the piece twice: once to get the overall meaning of the piece, and the second time to generate three words or associations that represent personal thoughts about the piece. Students then form groups of three and share their words. In groups, students negotiate their words and select the three words that best represent the piece. They then lay out and explain the three words that they have agreed on in the triangle organizer. Each student is invited to explain the connection between each pair of words and then to write a brief interpretation.

STEPS:

1. The teacher selects a text.

2. The teacher distributes triangle organizers so students can collect associations and develop connections.

3. After reading or listening to the piece twice, students generate three words that represent their thoughts about the piece.

4. Students form groups of three and share their three words. Students must agree on the three words that best represent the text.

5. Students lay out and explain the three words they have agreed upon in their triangle organizer.

6. Each student explains the connection between each pair of words.

7. Each student writes a brief interpretation.

Example: *A Fourth Grader's Associations for the Fable "Androclus and the Lion."*

Title _____ Androclus and the Lion _____

My three words

_____ Androclus _____

_____ help _____

_____ friends _____

Agreed upon words

_____ ran away _____

_____ help _____

_____ friends _____

Explanation

Androclus and the lion became friends. When
Androclus was captured, the
Romans put him in a stadium
with a hungry lion. But it was
the same lion. The lion
wouldn't kill Androclus because they were <u>friends</u>.

Ran away

Explanation

Androclus was a slave. His
master was mean and cruel. So
he <u>ran away</u>.

Friends

Help

Explanation

Androclus <u>helped</u> a lion by
pulling a thorn out of his paw.

My interpretation of the text

I think "Androclus and the Lion" is teaching us that we need to be kind to each
other. Androclus's master was mean, so Androclus ran away. Androclus was nice
to the lion, so the lion wouldn't kill him later on. If you are nice to others, they
will be nice to you.

Associations Organizer

Title_____

My three words   Agreed upon words

_____   _____

_____   _____

_____   _____

Explanation   Explanation

Explanation

My interpretation of the text

K.W.L. (Know-Want-Learn)

Purpose: This tool, designed by Ogle (1986) is used to assess students' prior knowledge, to help students generate questions about what they want to learn, and to encourage reflection upon what they have learned.

Procedure: The teacher introduces the topic to be studied, asking students to generate a list of what they already know about the topic. (Often, students do this individually, then in small groups, and finally, with the entire class.) After completing a concept map, the students generate a list outlining what they want to know. After generating this list, the students are engaged in instructional activities to help them find answers to their questions. After the instructional phase, the students reflect upon what they have learned, or what questions they were able to answer, and write this information in the "Learned" column of the K-W-L organizer.

A variation of K.W.L. has students generate responses to what they know, what they think they know, how they feel, and what they want to know. These additions (What do you think you know? How do you feel?) provide students with an opportunity to share their tentative knowledge and their feelings about the topic. They then can verify not only what they know, but decide if what they think they know can be moved to the "Know" column. By asking students how/what they feel, the teacher can monitor and assess any changes in affect toward the topic.

STEPS:

1. The teacher introduces the topic.

2. Students generate a list of what they know individually, in small groups, and then in a large group.

3. Students generate a list of questions about what they want to know.

4. The teacher provides a variety of learning opportunities (e.g., reading, video, lecture, lab, etc.) for students to acquire new information and address their questions.

5. Students add what they have learned to the "Learned" column, and then reflect upon the process.

          (c) 2001, The Thoughtful Education Press
(800) 962-4432

Example: *K-W-L for a Middle-School Unit on the Age of Exploration*

Before you begin this unit on explorers, take some time to think about what you already know about the Age of Exploration. Use the word bank below to help you. These words are not all the words you will come across during this unit, but they are some of the most commonly used when people talk about the Age of Exploration.

explorers	Christopher Columbus	conquistadores
sailors	Native Americans	The New World
maps	high seas	The Far East
India	navigation	Spain
Portugal	trade routes	voyage
discovery	spices	gold

Now, complete columns 1 & 2 below. Over the course of the unit, list what you've learned in the third column.

What do I know for sure about the Age of Exploration?	What do I want to learn or need to know about the Age of Exploration?	What have I learned about the Age of Exploration?

(c) 2001, The Thoughtful Education Press
(800) 962-4432

Four Thought

Purpose: A tool designed to help students use their pre-reading thoughts and feelings and their post-reading insights to develop deep and layered interpretations.

Procedure: Four Thought begins with the teacher introducing the topic and asking students to generate any thoughts and feelings they have about the topic. The teacher provides a reading for students and a Four Thought organizer which asks students to describe the topic or situation, analyze it, apply a solution, and react personally. (Alternatively, the organizer can contain items that ask students to develop a sequence, draw a comparison, make an evaluation, develop a metaphor, create an icon or picture, explain the value of the topic, etc.) Students respond to each of the Four Thought stems once they have completed the reading. In groups, students share their responses and exchange ideas for turning their Four Thought into an essay on the topic. Once the first draft is complete, students work in Writer's Clubs (see pg. 84) to obtain feedback on the clarity of the writing, use of powerful words or phrases, coherence of sentences, use of all the Four Thought stems in the response, and writing mechanics. Students use this feedback to revise and polish their essays.

STEPS:

1. The teacher selects a topic or text and prepares a Four Thought organizer.

2. The teacher introduces students to the four thinking stems (describe, analyze, apply, react).

3. Students generate initial associations.

4. Students respond to each of the Four Thought stems.

5. Students meet with other students to share their responses.

6. Students use their Four Thoughts to write a first draft of an essay on the topic.

7. Students form writing clubs to provide feedback focused on powerful words, clarity of writing, use of four thought stems, and writing conventions.

8. Students reflect on what they have learned and revise their initial draft.

 (c) 2001, The Thoughtful Education Press
(800) 962-4432

Example: *A High-School Student's Four Thoughts on Elephant Endangerment*

Topic: _____ Endangered Elephants in Africa _____

Pre-reading Associations

Africa	ivory	ecosystem
hunters	environment	vulnerable
greed	Green Peace	World Wildlife Fund
money	profits	

FourThought

Describe it	React to it
Elephants are being killed by poachers. They are killed for their ivory tusks, which are in demand as a material for making jewelry.	I feel almost guilty living in a society that would put luxury over the extinction of a species. To me, life is more precious than ivory or art or profit, and I would like to know what gives people the right to hunt a species to virtual extinction for a mere luxury.
Analyze it	**Solve it**
The poachers' livelihoods depend on ivory. The poachers who kill the wild African elephants do so to earn money to feed and clothe themselves and their families. However, is poaching the only answer to their economic needs?	The first step in solving this problem is to educate the public. There are millions of people who have never even heard of the wild African elephant. If they knew about this situation, I'm sure many of them would be sympathetic. The second step would be to find another way for the poachers to make money. Maybe they could set up government jobs for them to turn to instead of killing.

Four Thought Organizer

Topic:_____

Pre-reading Associations

FourThought

Describe it	React to it
Analyze it	**Solve it**

Alternative Four Thought Stems:

Instead of *describing it*, students can *define it* or *sequence it*.

Instead of *analyzing it*, students can *compare it* or *prove it*.

Instead of *solving it*, students can *visualize/metaphorize it* or *improve it*.

Instead of *reacting to it*, students can *be it* or *teach it*.

Think of A Time
(Point of View Strategy)

Purpose: This technique, based on the work of Fay Brownlie and Susan Close (1992) is designed to help students see content from different points of view.

Procedure: Students are grouped into threes and numbered one, two, and three. Students are asked to examine an issue from three points of view:

1. As a "participant";
2. As an "observer";
3. As a "supporter."

In the first round, the teacher asks students to think of a time when they were participants in something related to the content they are being taught (e.g., when they were confronted with prejudice). Students record what they remember about the experience in writing. They then compare their stories with others in their group to determine common attributes. After exploring the various points of view in their group, the number one students move to another group where they summarize their original group's ideas. The new group listens and compares its ideas with the new ideas.

The process is then repeated from the second perspective. The teacher asks the students to think of a time when they were an observer (e.g., when they observed someone confronted with prejudice). Students record and discuss in a similar manner. Then, number two students move to a new group and discuss in the same manner as the first round.

Finally, students are asked to consider the experience from the third perspective--what it was like when they supported someone (e.g., when they supported someone who was experiencing prejudice). Students record and discuss. Then, number three students move to a new group.

The last group develops a set of attributes or elements critical to the concept being examined. The students reflect upon what they know about the concept and what they noticed about themselves as learners. They then establish goals for deepening their understanding the next time they engage in the process.

STEPS:

1. Students are grouped into threes, and each student is assigned a number (1, 2, 3).

2. Students examine an issue from three points of view:
   - Participant   - Observer   - Supporter

3. Students respond individually in writing, comparing their stories with others and examining common attributes (3x - one for each point of view).

4. After exploring each point of view, one student from each group joins a new group, where he/she shares the original group's attributes with the new group.

5. The last triad develops a set of attributes or elements critical to the concept being examined.

6. The students reflect upon what new insights they have that they didn't have when the process started. They also reflect upon themselves as learners and establish a goal for the next time that will allow them to deepen their engagement in the process.

Example: *Think of a time when you exhibited courage. Think of a time when you observed someone being courageous. Think of a time when you helped someone to be courageous.*

A variation of this strategy is to select an issue and have students explain it from three points of view.

Examples: *Explain the westward movement from the point of view of the settlers, the Indians, and the trappers. Explain biogenetics from the point of view of a minister, a doctor, and a scientist.*

Hooks & Bridges

Purpose: Techniques used to get students thinking about the content, to provide a natural entryway into a new topic, and to connect new information to what is already known.

Procedure: A hook focuses thinking and opens up memory banks closely associated with the new topic. In creating a hook, the teacher should look for themes or concepts that unite the material and for a way to use these themes to grab students' attention. There are four different types of hooks teachers can use:

Mastery hooks ask students to recall what they already know about the topic.

Understanding hooks ask students to examine data and extract principles.

Self-Expressive hooks ask students to use metaphors or "What if" queries to harness the imagination in preparing for the lesson.

Interpersonal hooks ask students to use their own feelings and experiences to lay the groundwork for the lesson.

In hooking students to new material, you should rotate the styles of your hooks so as to engage all your students.

After you have given students time to process, respond to, and discuss the hook, you are ready to bridge the hook to the content. To bridge prior knowledge to the new lesson, the teacher simply shows students how the ideas they came up with are related to the new material. This can be done by making a statement or posing a question.

STEPS:

1. The teacher presents students with a question that will generate interest and focus thinking (Hook).

2. Students respond individually, in groups, and/or as an entire class (see *Kindling,* pg. 74 for an effective response technique).

3. The teacher and students discuss responses.

4. The teacher asks a question or makes a statement to connect new material with the hook (BRIDGE).

5. The teacher begins the lesson or lecture with students already engaged and focused.

Example: *Four Hooks and Bridges*

Mastery Hook	Interpersonal Hook
Hook: Think for a minute about anything you know about the circulatory system. What do you know about blood and how it moves through the body?	**Hook:** Think back on a time when you were really scared. What caused you to get scared?
Bridge: Good! You really know a lot about circulation. Now let's build some new information on what you already know.	**Bridge:** Good! You've described the way fear can grow. Let's look at how a great writer makes our fear grow.
Understanding Hook	**Self-Expressive Hook**
Hook: Here are two subtraction problems that use borrowing and two that don't. What differences do you notice? Why might there be these differences?	**Hook:** Imagine that you came back to America 300 years later and discovered that it was no longer a great power. What do you suppose caused this change of power?
Bridge: Good! Now let me show you some subtraction problems, and we'll see which of your ideas are true.	**Bridge:** Good! Now let's see what caused the fall of the Roman Empire.

Tools for
Focusing Learning

Anticipation Guide

Purpose: A technique adapted from the work of Herber (1970) that is used to prepare readers by asking them to react to a series of statements related to the content. The purpose of the guide is to get students to anticipate or predict what content they will be reading. Anticipation Guides help students to connect what they already know with new information they are about to learn; moreover, they help to establish interest in the topic and involve students in discussion after the reading.

Procedure: The teacher first reviews the text, video, or demonstration, then the major concepts. After deciding which concepts are most likely to stimulate student background knowledge, the teacher prepares three to five statements based on the key concepts. General statements work better than specific statements. The statements are provided to the students before they read the text, and students are asked to decide which statements they believe the text will support. Students should talk through their opinions with other students. The teacher then prepares a class tally for each statement, discusses student responses, and asks for elaboration and substantiation. Next, students read the text and collect information to support or refute the statement. Finally, students compare their original responses to their new ideas, which have been informed by the text.

STEPS:

1. The teacher identifies major concepts in a text, video, or demonstration.

2. The teacher establishes three to five statements and develops an Anticipation Guide.

3. Students respond to the statements one at a time.

4. The teacher develops a class tally for each statement and discusses opinions. The teacher should use Q-SPACE for students to clarify, substantiate, and elaborate upon their responses (See Q-SPACE, pg. 122)

5. Students read the text and collect information to support or refute statements.

6. Students compare their original responses with those they generate after reading.

7. Students reflect upon the process.

The Origin of the Universe

BEFORE READING				AFTER READING	
Agree	**Disagree**			**Agree**	**Disagree**

_____   _____   1.   People have come up with many myths and theories about the origin of the universe.   _____   _____

_____   _____   2.   Cosmologists and scientists tend not to agree on one explanation about the origin of the cosmos.   _____   _____

_____   _____   3.   The Big Bang theory contends that all the material and energy in our present universe once existed in an atomized single particle.   _____   _____

_____   _____   4.   Mathematics has been used to prove that the galaxies all began at a single point and are spreading apart at a terrific rate of speed.   _____   _____

_____   _____   5.   The evidence to support the Big Bang theory is conclusive.   _____   _____

Word Banks

Purpose: A technique used to minimize students' need to remember information, while enhancing their ability to demonstrate their comprehension. Word banks reduce the burden of memorizing by providing students with the names of the concepts they will be using in the assessment.

Procedure: The teacher identifies key ideas related to the content being studied and presents them to the students, usually in an alphabetical word list. The teacher then assigns a task for students to complete (e.g., completing an organizer, filling in answers to questions, constructing a response to a question). Since the students have access to the key words, the focus is not on trying to remember the ideas, but on knowing the concepts and using them appropriately. This tool is a good technique to accommodate students with special needs and those who have memory problems.

STEPS:

1. The teacher reviews text and identifies key concepts.

2. The teacher presents a word bank to students.

3. Students use word bank to complete a task.

4. The teacher and students review assignment and evaluate comprehension.

Example: *A Word Bank in Basic Geometry*

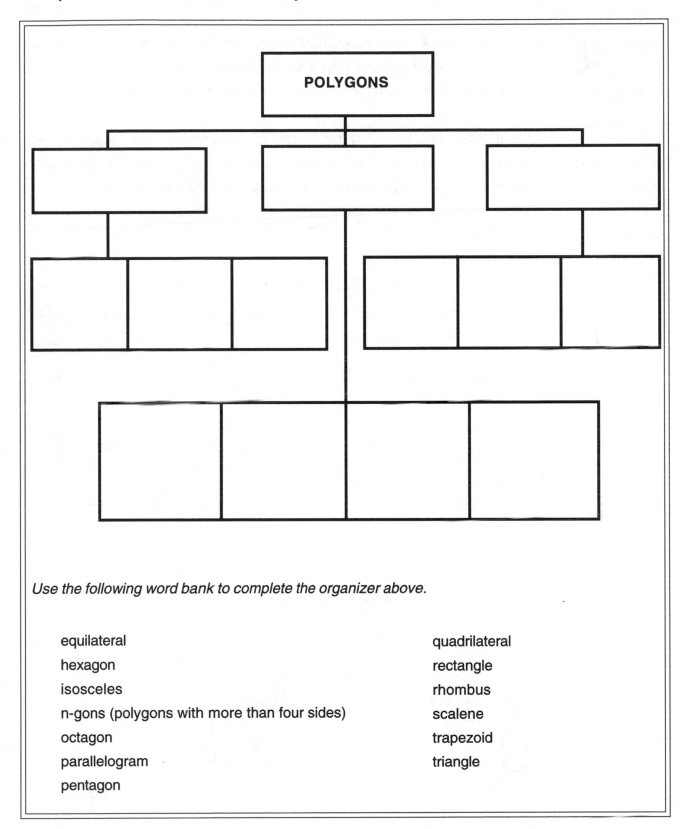

Use the following word bank to complete the organizer above.

equilateral   quadrilateral

hexagon   rectangle

isosceles   rhombus

n-gons (polygons with more than four sides)   scalene

octagon   trapezoid

parallelogram   triangle

pentagon

(c) 2001, The Thoughtful Education Press
(800) 962-4432

Sketch-To-Stretch

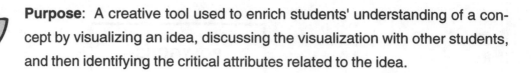

Purpose: A creative tool used to enrich students' understanding of a concept by visualizing an idea, discussing the visualization with other students, and then identifying the critical attributes related to the idea.

Procedure: Following the presentation of new information, the students are asked to draw a picture or set of icons that represent their understanding of the concept. After the students complete their visualization, they meet with one or two other students to discuss their pictures. After the discussion, the students work alone, listing what they believe are the big ideas and important details.

STEPS:

1.   After new information is presented, students convert their understanding of the concept into a picture or set of icons.

2.   Students form groups of two or three to review and discuss their visualizations.

3.   After discussing their pictures, the students work alone, listing what they believe to be the big ideas and important details.

Example: *Sketch-to-Stretch for a Reading on the Big Bang*

Directions: As you read the passage on the Big Bang that follows, stop and draw sketches that remind you of the big ideas and important details in the reading. Avoid using any written language in your sketches. Just "picture" the information. A sketch area is provided to the right of the reading.

Reading

How did galaxies, stars, and our sun come to be? This fundamental question has probably been with us for all time. People have come up with many myths and theories to answer it. Cosmologists, scientists who study this question, tend to agree on one explanation that makes the most sense based on careful observations. This explanation is called the Big Bang Theory.

According to the Big Bang Theory, all of the material and energy of our present universe once existed as an atom-sized singularity. Obviously, something so small yet so packed with material and energy had to be very dense. It is difficult for physicists to describe the conditions that immediately followed. 15 to 20 billion years ago, an explosion of unimaginable force occurred in this singularity. Evidence for this explosion comes from spectroscopic data which tells us that the galaxies are spreading apart at a terrific rate of speed. If we note the present location of galaxies and mathematically retrace their paths, we find that they all began at a single point and time . . . the time of the Big Bang.

The explosion sent matter flying out in all directions at nearly the speed of light. The temperature was incredible. Within minutes the matter cooled enough for subatomic particles to form simple hydrogen and helium atoms. These gases continued to expand and cool.

Clumps of gas condensed, eventually forming galaxies. Our galaxy, formed in this way, is called the Milky Way. It contains about 2000 billion stars. About one-third of the way in from the edge of the galaxy was a spinning cloud of gas and dust. This cloud would eventually become the sun.

Sketch Area

(c) 2001, The Thoughtful Education Press
(800) 962-4432

Mind's Eye

Purpose: A technique developed by Brownlie and Silver (1995) that is used to engage students in pre-reading by having them create images in their mind while listening to key words from the text.

Procedure: The teacher reviews the text the students will read and identifies 20 to 30 key words. The teacher then asks the students to decide if they are more likely to draw a picture, ask a question, make a prediction, or express a feeling. The teacher reads the list of words slowly, with emphasized emotion. As she reads each word, she encourages the students to create pictures in their minds about the story and, with each word, to add to their initial pictures. After the teacher completes all the words, the students are given four choices:

- Draw a picture of the story
- Ask a question about the story
- Make a prediction about the story
- Describe a feeling they have about the story

The students are invited to share their products. The teacher then has the students read the text. As they read, they compare their initial ideas about the story with the actual story.

STEPS:

1. The teacher selects 20 to 30 key words from the text students will read.

2. The students are asked to predict if they are more likely to:
   - Draw a picture
   - Ask a question
   - Make a prediction
   - Describe a feeling

3. The teacher then reads the words to the students one at a time, slowly, with emotion.

4. As the teacher reads the words, the students construct mental pictures in their minds.

     (c) 2001, The Thoughtful Education Press
(800) 962-4432

5. When the teacher completes the list of words, the students select one of the four choices.

6. The students share their products and compare their initial ideas about the story with the reading of the text.

7. The students reflect upon the process and the types of thinking they are most comfortable using.

Example: *Mind's Eye for* A Tale of Two Cities

To help students visualize and make predictions about Chapter VII of Dickens' *A Tale of Two Cities*, the teacher reads these key words aloud:

storm, snuff, downstairs, courtyard, carriage, dispersed, horses, escaping, recklessness, narrow, streets, screaming, loud, cry, wrong, child, killed, shrieked, desperation, eyes, watchfulness, purse, coin, dead, silent, pay, dignity, contemptuous, "Go on!", fancy, ball, knitting.

Picture	Feeling
Question	**Prediction**

(c) 2001, The Thoughtful Education Press
(800) 962-4432

Tools for Improving Student Decision Making

Priority Pyramid

Purpose: A technique that helps students prioritize ideas according to what their personal values.

Procedure: The teacher provides students with a list of items and a pyramid organizer to record them. Alternatively, students can generate their own list, or items can be taken from a text (e.g., students pick the five most important ideas from a passage). Students should place the most important idea on the top, the next most important idea on the next tier, etc., until the last item is put at the base of the pyramid. After the students have ranked the items, they should reflect on their choices and try to identify the criteria they used to determine the rank order.

STEPS:

1. The teacher provides the students with a pyramid organizer.

2. The teacher provides a list of items (or the students can select their own). The teacher explains that the most important idea is placed at the top of the pyramid, followed by the next idea, etc., so that the least important idea is at the base of the pyramid.

3. Students examine items on the list or in the text and rank them according to importance.

4. Students reflect upon their choices and identify the criteria they used to determine the rankings.

Example: *A Student's Priority Pyramid on Personal Values*

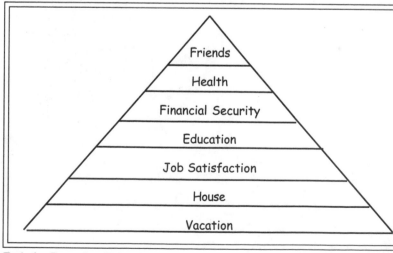

I focused on two main criteria: personal happiness and health. All of the other things are important, but without personal happiness and health, they're not worth very much.

I chose friends first because for me, they're the ultimate source of personal happiness.

(c) 2001, The Thoughtful Education Press
(800) 962-4432

Rank Order Ladder

Purpose: A technique used to help students sequence items according to a set of objective criteria.

Procedure: Unlike the Priority Pyramid, for the Rank Order Ladder the teacher will establish objective criteria for organizing the information (quantity, time, order, etc.). The students need to know the order according to these criteria. For example, students can be asked to put four documents in order (e.g., Declaration of Independence, Mayflower Compact, Articles of Confederation, Magna Carta) and explain their relationship according to the principles of American democracy.

STEPS:

1. The teacher establishes the items and objective criteria (e.g., time, quantity, size, etc.) by which students should order the items.

2. The teacher provides items, or students select items to be ranked.

3. Students rank items and explain how they used the criteria to obtain their order.

Example: *Rank the following countries in terms of total population: China, Russia, United States, India, Indonesia, Mexico, and Japan. Now rank them according to size.*
Which nation do you think has the most pronounced population problem? Why?

Decision-Making Matrix

Purpose: A tool to help students systematically analyze and choose among alternatives.

Procedure: The teacher provides students with a matrix organizer. On one side of the matrix, they list the alternatives that will be analyzed. On the other side, they list the specific attributes they will consider in choosing among the alternatives. For each attribute, students determine its weight of importance (3=very important, 2=important, 1=not as important).

Next, students analyze each alternative against each attribute. After analyzing each attribute, they multiply the score according to its weight of importance. Once they have completed their determination, they decide if they want to change any scores. After reviewing their scores, students compute a total score for each alternative. They then compare their analytical score with how they feel about their choice. If it fits, great; if not, students reevaluate their scores until their analysis and feelings are aligned.

STEPS:

1. The teacher or student identifies the alternatives to be examined.

2. A matrix organizer is used to analyze the alternatives. Students list alternatives on the top.

3. The teacher or students identify the attributes that will be used to analyze the alternatives and list them along the side of the matrix.

4. Students determine the weight of importance of each attribute (3=very important, 2=important, 1=not as important).

5. Students analyze each alternative against each attribute (meets this attribute: 3=completely, 2=to a great extent, 1=somewhat, 0=not at all).

6. Students compute the score for each alternative by multiplying the weighted score and attribute rating. They then total the attribute score for each alternative.

7. Students identify the alternative with the highest score. Does it match their feelings about which alternative to choose? If so, great; if not, they reevaluate the attributes, the importance, and the ratings. They continue to reevaluate until they are comfortable with their choice.

Example: *A Student's Decision-Making Matrix for Selecting a Bicycle*

Rating Scale
3=completely
2=considerably
1=somewhat
0=not at all

Attributes	Importance	Peugeot	Bianchi	Raleigh
Price	3	2 x 3 = 6	1 x 3 = 3	3 x 3 = 9
Weight	1	2 x 1 = 2	3 x 1 = 3	1 x 1 = 1
Shifting Ease	2	3 x 2 = 6	3 x 2 = 6	2 x 2 = 4
Handling	3	2 x 3 = 6	2 x 3 = 6	2 x 3 = 6
Comfort	2	2 x 2 = 4	3 x 2 = 6	1 x 2 = 2
Style	1	2 x 1 = 2	3 x 1 = 3	2 x 1 = 2
Total Score		27	26	24

Physical Barometer

Purpose: A technique for assessing students' positions quickly and for having students participate physically in the lesson.

Procedure: The teacher designates specific areas in the classroom to represent various positions (e.g., strongly agree, agree, neutral, disagree, and strongly disagree). The teacher then makes a statement or poses a question like: *Should animal testing be allowed in scientific research?*

The students think about the statement or question, get up from their seats, and move to the part of the room that reflects their position or answer. The students first discuss the reasons for their choice with other students who have taken the same position. They then explain their position to the rest of the class. The groups can ask questions of each other. After the question and answer period, the students are asked to reflect again and then to take a final position (either stay where they are or move). Students who choose to move should be prepared to explain why they moved. Often, a writing activity follows.

STEPS:

1. The teacher designates areas of the room to represent distinct positions/responses to a question.

2. The teacher poses a question or makes a statement.

3. Students reflect on the issue or question, take a position, and move to the appropriate region of the classroom.

4. Students discuss the rationale for their position with others who have the same position.

5. Students in each group explain/defend their position to the rest of the class.

6. Students reflect on their choice and ask questions of each other.

7. Students take a final position and defend their choice either verbally, or more commonly, in writing.

(c) 2001, The Thoughtful Education Press
(800) 962-4432

Tools for Building Students' Notemaking Skills

New American Notebook

Purpose: A notemaking and study technique to help students extract meaningful information from reading and recall information accurately. The method includes anticipating what will be read, reading with a purpose, and reviewing and recalling what is important.

Process: New American Notebook (adapted from Pauk, 1974) involves the teacher and/or students in surveying the text in order to preview what the students will be reading. This can be done by reading the bold face, topic sentences, summary paragraphs, or review questions. Then, students generate questions they think the text will answer. An easy way to create questions is for the students to turn the boldface type or the topic sentences into questions. Students read one section of the text at a time. As they read, they collect and record the big ideas and important details necessary to answer each question they have generated. When it comes time to review, students survey the question(s) and response(s) to determine if they understand the answer, still have some questions, or need further review. Often they use a set of reader's punctuation ($\sqrt{}$ = I know this, ? = I have a question about this, * = I need to review this).

To review, students cover their notes, read each question, and attempt to recite the answer. They then proceed to the next section of the text, repeating the process. After the students have finished reading and answering all the questions, they go over their notes to get a comprehensive grasp of the complete assignment.

STEPS:

1. The teacher and student preview the text and read the topic headings, the summary paragraphs, and the review questions at the end of the chapter.

2. Students turn the topic headings into questions.

3. Students read the text carefully, one section at a time, looking for the big ideas and important details related to each question.

4. Students review each question and determine if they understand the answer, have any questions, or need further review, using a set of reader's punctuation:

   $\sqrt{}$ = I know this
   ? = I have a question about this
   * = I need to review this

5. Students answer the questions without looking at their notes or the text.

6.   After they have finished answering the questions, students go on to the next section of the assignment.

7.   Once the assignment is finished, students put the book down and review their notes in order to get a comprehensive grasp of the complete assignment.

Example: *New American Notes on the Circulatory System*

The Circulatory System: Blood

Questions	Main Ideas	Details	Monitor
1. What is the function of blood?	Brings food and oxygen to cells and carries away wastes. It moves enzymes and infection fighters.	Food gets picked up at small intestine, oxygen at lungs, wastes go to kidneys.	
2. What are the parts of the blood, and what are their functions?	Plasma-mostly water; does most carrying.	55% of blood	
	Red cells-hemoglobin to pick up oxygen.	No nuclei, made in bone marrow.	
	White cells-fight microorganisms and clear dead cells.	Have nucleus, made in marrow and lymph nodes. 1 white per 650 red.	
3. How do platelets stop bleeding?	Break up and form fibrin with help of broken vessels. Fibrin makes nets of scabs.		

Monitor:

√ = I know this!
? = Question
* = Need review

(c) 2001, The Thoughtful Education Press
(800) 962-4432

Mapping

Purpose: A technique (sometimes called mind mapping or webbing) used to create visual representations of hierarchical relationships between a central concept, supporting ideas, and important details. Mapping can be used to teach vocabulary, to introduce outlining, to teach note-taking, to foster pre-reading comprehension, to demonstrate comprehension, or to help students study.

Procedure: The first step in developing a map is for the teacher or students to identify a topic, main idea, or central question. The students write the central concept in a circle on the center of their page. The secondary categories are identified and connected to the main idea. The students then either generate or collect supporting details. The supporting details are connected to the idea or topic they support.

Maps force students to pay attention through reading, recalling, and studying. In addition, they make explicit the hierarchical patterns of comprehension. Mapping the entire chapter of a text, however, may be too time-consuming; it may be best to map a significant portion of a chapter.

STEPS:

1. Students identify the topic, main idea, or central question, write it in the center of the page, and circle it.

2. The teacher or student identifies secondary categories (may be chapter headings in the text). Secondary categories are connected to the main idea.

3. Students collect or generate supporting details and connect them to the categories they support. The process continues until all notes are connected to other notes in a way that makes sense.

(c) 2001, The Thoughtful Education Press
(800) 962-4432

Example: *Mapping the States of Matter*

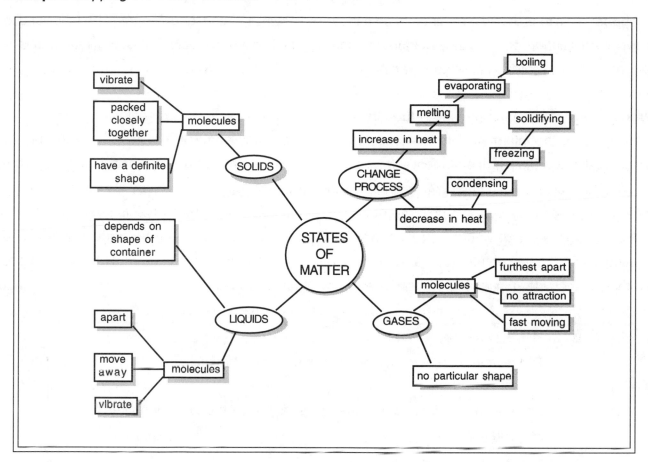

Etch-A-Sketch

Purpose: This tool, based on a strategy developed by Brownlie, Close, and Wingren (1990) is used to present information and enhance student memory. Students draw symbols, icons, or pictures to represent ideas presented in a lecture, reading, or other form of presentation.

Procedure: The teacher provides students with a brief overview of the presentation. The teacher then presents the information to the students, speaking slowly and with emotion. As the teacher presents the information, the students draw pictures or icons to represent their understanding of the ideas. The students then meet with each other and compare their pictures. They are asked to guess what each other's icons or symbols represent. After the discussion, the students record what they believe to be the big ideas and important details. The teacher then collects the students' ideas and continues with the presentation of the lecture. At the end of the presentation, the students are asked to synthesize their ideas in writing, visual format, or a combination of both.

─── STEPS: ───

1. The teacher presents an overview of the presentation.

2. Students draw pictures or icons of the lecture as the teacher makes the presentation.

3. The teacher pauses regularly to allow students to complete their visualizations.

4. The students then meet with a partner to examine their pictures. Each student tries to guess what the symbols represent.

5. After reviewing their pictures, the students record what they believe to be the big ideas and important details.

6. The teacher leads a discussion of the ideas presented.

7. After the discussion, the teacher continues with the lecture, pausing regularly to allow students to process their ideas.

Example: *Etch-A-Sketch for Jonathan Edwards' Sermon, "Sinners in the Hands of an Angry God"*

Topic	SINNERS IN THE HANDS OF AN ANGRY GOD

	Sketch	**Big Ideas and Important Details**
1		- man can die at any moment and be damned without knowing where or when death and damnation will come.
2		- the hand of God is the only thing holding back sin and the devil from getting at man.
3		- God's mercy and grace are arbitrary.

(c) 2001, The Thoughtful Education Press
(800) 962-4432

Etch-A-Sketch Worksheet

Topic _____

	Sketch	Big Ideas and Important Details
1		
2		
3		

Power Notes

Purpose: A simplified outlining procedure that teaches students how to organize their readings according to the "power" of the ideas they contain.

Procedure: Power Notes (Sparks, 1982) teaches students how to organize information into a simple outline with various levels or "powers" of specificity. It is based on the Arabic numbers 1, 2, 3, and 4 rather than the traditional Roman numerals of I, II, III, and IV. Power 1 ideas are the main ideas. Powers 2, 3, and 4 contain information that is increasingly specific.

STEPS:

1. The teacher demonstrates how to use Power Notes by modeling an easy topic with a clear structure.

2. The teacher explains the concept of powers by showing students how they can add increasingly specific levels of information.

3. The teacher and students create Power Note models as a class, using topics students are comfortable with (e.g., foods, movies, hobbies, jobs).

4. Students practice organizing the ideas in their readings using Power Notes.

5. The teacher allows for more and more individual work as students gain proficiency.

Example: *Power Notes for a Reading on Resistive Forces*

On the previous pages, you discovered and studied the three resistive forces. In the past you may have called them by another name or described them differently, but in physics the three resistive forces are called *gravity, inertia,* and *friction.*

Gravity is the force that attracts two objects to each other. The more massive the objects and the closer they are to each other, the stronger the force of gravity. Because the earth is so massive, we must work to lift objects and ourselves up and away from the earth and its gravity.

Inertia is the resistance of objects to changes in speed or direction, even if the speed is zero. The more massive an object is, the more difficult it is to get it to speed up, slow down, or even turn! For example, when pushing a car, the first second or two is the hardest as you must first overcome the massive car's inertia. It will be equally hard to bring the car to a stop later.

The third resistive force is friction. Friction is the force that tries to stop motion when two objects rub against each other. Friction happens because the molecules of each substance grip each other. The harder they are pressed against each other, the harder the grip. Most lubricants are liquids that create a space between two objects that would otherwise scrape against each other and cause friction.

It's the three resistive forces--*gravity, inertia, and friction*--that make work so hard!

Topic: Resistive Forces

Power 1: Gravity
  Power 2: Force that attracts two objects together.
    Power 3: The bigger the objects and closer they are to each other, the stronger the force of gravity.
      Power 4: It takes work to lift an object because the Earth's mass creates a lot of gravity.

Power 1: Inertia
  Power 2: Resistance of object to change in speed or direction, even if the speed is zero.
    Power 3: More massive objects are harder to speed up, slow down, and turn.
      Power 4: It takes more work to start a car moving and to stop it than it takes to keep it in motion.

Power 1: Friction
  Power 2: Force that tries to stop motion when two objects rub against each other.
    Power 3: Friction happens when the molecules of two substances grip each other.
      Power 4: Lubricants are liquids that reduce the friction between objects.

Math Notes

Purpose: A tool used to teach students how to use notemaking to examine the components of word problems and to develop thoughtful solutions.

Procedure: Word problems are a source of difficulty for many math students. Suddenly, math students have to become careful readers and determine how to set up the problem for themselves. What students need is a systematic way to gather the facts, determine the question, represent the problem, and think through the steps that will yield a solution.

To use Math Notes, the teacher chooses a word problem. Using a blank Math Notes organizer, the teacher helps the students identify the facts of the problem and decide what is missing. Students determine the main question that needs answering and search for hidden questions and assumptions. Next, the students look for a visual way to represent the problem and sketch it. Students identify what steps need to be taken to solve the problem and then solve it on the bottom of their organizer.

It is a good idea to have students keep a notebook of all the problems they solve using Math Notes. That way, when they encounter new problems, they can refer to their notebooks and look for methods they used to solve similar problems.

STEPS:

1. Using a blank Math Notes organizer, the teacher models an example, allowing the students to hear the thinking out loud while breaking the problem down into:

· The Facts	Identify the facts of the problem and decide what is missing.
· The Question	Determine the main question that needs answering and search for hidden questions and assumptions.
· The Diagram	Sketch a visual representation of the problem.
· The Steps	Decide what steps need to be taken to solve the problem.

2. Students practice solving problems using Math Notes and collect their work in a problem-solving notebook.

3. As students encounter new problems, they review their notebooks and look for effective problem-solving models.

(c) 2001, The Thoughtful Education Press
(800) 962-4432

Example: *Math Notes in Fourth Grade*

The Problem: *There are six fourth-grade classes in Joyce Kilmer Elementary school. All the classes have 24 students, except for one, which has 25 students. All the fourth-grade students are going on a field trip to the zoo. If vans hold eight students and buses hold 45, determine how many buses and how many vans will be needed to transport all the fourth-graders to the zoo.*

The Facts

What are the facts?
-Vans hold 8 people.
- Buses hold 45 people.

What is missing?
-Number of kids in 4th grade.
-Number of vans and buses grade 4 needs.

The Steps

What steps can we take to solve the problem?

-Find out how many people are going on the trip.
-See how many will fit in buses because buses hold more people and fewer vehicles make less pollution for the environment.
-Put the leftovers in vans.
-Count the number of vehicles we used.

The Question

What question needs to be answered?
-How many vans and buses does our grade need?

Are there any hidden questions that need to be answered?
-How many people are going on the trip?
-Are empty seats ok?
-Should each vehicle be full?

The Diagram

How can we represent the problem visually?

 = 8

 = 145

 = 45

Math Notes Organizer

The Facts	The Steps
What are the facts? **What is missing?**	**What steps can we take to solve the problem?**

The Question	The Diagram
What question needs to be answered? **Are there any hidden questions that need to be answered?**	**How can we represent the problem visually?**

The Solution

Concept Notemaker

Purpose: A notemaking and study technique to help students collect important information about a concept. The method includes a set of critical questions that guide students in their collection and organization of information.

Process: The Concept Notemaker provides students with a critical set of questions to guide them in their examination of any important concept. The questions to be addressed are:

- What is the concept?
- What does it look like?
- What are its parts?
- What is its purpose?
- How does it operate?
- How did it originate?
- What is it part of?
- What is its importance?

After the students have collected the necessary information about the concept they are working with, they can synthesize the information into a narrative, visual, or metaphoric form.

STEPS:

1. The teacher provides students with a concept to research and a Concept Notemaker form for collecting information.

2. Students read and research the concept they are studying.

3. As student read and research, they record the information on their Concept Notemaker organizer.

4. Students share their information they have collected with others, and correct and clarify their ideas.

5. Students then synthesize the information they have collected and transform it into a narrative, visualization, or metaphor.

Concept Notemaker Organizer

Content to be examined: (Resources used)

What does it look like?

What are its parts?

What is its purpose?

How does it operate?

How did it originate?

What is it part of?

What is its importance?

Tools for Improving Student Writing

Learning Log

Purpose: A strategy to record student ideas related to the content they are learning. A Learning Log is an active response journal for recording information, reactions, thoughts, and feelings. It is a multidimensional tool for checking student understanding of the content; for expanding student thinking and reflection; for getting students to generate new ideas, think creatively, make personal connections, and clarify thoughts and feelings. Learning Logs help students retain and make sense of information. They also help students improve the communication skills of writing, listening, and speaking.

Procedure: The teacher asks students to write their ideas in response to a question or after a period of learning information. Students write for an identified period of time (often 3-5 minutes) in a notebook identified as their log. Students may respond with personal connections, creative ideas, paraphrases, or responses to learning. Below are some basic guidelines and ideas for using Learning Logs productively:

- A Learning Log can be anything from a marble-colored composition book to a special section of your notebook.
- A Learning Log is a place where students keep "provisional" and "readable" writing.
- A Learning Log is a place where students record their thoughts about content.
- Writing in Learning Logs may be used for evaluation or not, at the teacher's discretion.
- Every other week, students should receive at least one or two personal responses from the teacher to their writing. To make this neat and manageable, students should label every fourth page "Comments."
- Teachers can keep their own logs and share responses with students.
- Teachers should model responses initially.
- Students can be given Question Menus (see pg. 128) and can choose the best way to respond.
- When working on Building Writing Questions (see pg. 76), students should write out the question they have chosen and the date.
- Learning Logs are not journals or diaries; they are not private. Other people (students, teachers, parents) can be encouraged to read and respond to Learning Logs.
- Comments in Learning Logs work best when they:
    1. Relate to specific ideas in students' writing.
    2. Raise questions.
    3. Express appreciation.

(c) 2001, The Thoughtful Education Press
(800) 962-4432

STEPS:

1. Students open their Learning Logs to write.

2. The teacher provides a prompt (or students may select a prompt or question themselves).

3. Students write for 3 to 5 minutes.

Example: *Think about what you know about cell division. Write down facts, thoughts, ideas, or other relevant information in your Learning Log.*

(c) 2001, The Thoughtful Education Press
(800) 962-4432

Kindling

Purpose: A writing technique that promotes sharing, deep thought, communication, and cooperative work.

Procedure: As with Think, Pair, Share (see pg. 10) the teacher poses a question for students to consider. Instead of sharing with neighbors, however, students jot down, scribble, or draw their responses in their Learning Logs. The students then share their ideas either with neighbors or with a small group. The students can compare their ideas with others, critique each other's ideas, generate new ideas, or draw conclusions from everyone's responses. The teacher collects and records students' ideas on the board so they can be examined and explored further.

STEPS:

1. The teacher poses a question.

2. Students think about the question.

3. Students record their ideas in their Learning Logs.

4. Students share their responses in pairs or small groups.

5. Students look for similarities between responses, critique ideas, generate new ideas, or draw conclusions.

6. The teacher collects and records ideas so they can be examined and explored further in class.

Compare & contrast:

To determine differences or similarities on the basis of certain criteria:
- List the similarities and differences.
- Compare and contrast the following_____.
- What are the significant similarities or differences between _____ and_____?
- Which two are most similar or most different?

Relate personally:

To describe emotional states/feelings or to connect learning to life and personal experience:
- What are your feelings about_____?
- How would you feel if_____happened to you?
- What would you do if_____happened to you?
- What are some possible feelings you had when that happened?

Evaluate:

To appraise the value or worth of a thing or idea to make a judgment concerning specific criteria:
- Which alternative would you choose and why?
- What are the advantages or disadvantages of_____?
- Given the following choices, justify or substantiate your selection.

Associate:

To relate objects/thoughts as they come to mind:
- What words/ideas come to mind when I say_____?
- What do you think of when you listen to the_____?
- What do you think of when you see the_____?

Trace/ sequence:

To arrange information in a logical order according to chronology, quantity, quality, or location:
- Trace the development of_____.
- Sequence the events leading up to_____.
- What do you do first when you_____?

Enumerate:

To list in concise form or to name one after another:
- List the causes of the _____.
- List the facts regarding_____.
- List the steps involved in_____.

Identify & describe:

To identify the properties of particular items, happenings or concepts:
- What did you see, hear, note?
- Describe the facts.
- What did you observe?
- Describe the characteristics or properties of the object.

Define:

To give the meaning of a word or concept:
- Define the following concept_____?
- Define what is meant by_____?
- Define the word from the context clues.

Explore & predict:

To generate alternatives and assumptions concerning cause and effect:
- How many ways can you_____?
- What would happen if_____?
- Suppose_____happened? What would be the consequences?

Argue a position:

To explain good reasons for a particular position; to present facts to support your position:
- Where do you stand on this issue?
- Justify your position.
- Explain your argument.
- What are your reasons for taking this position?

Summarize:

To state briefly or in conclusive form the substance of what has been observed, heard or experienced:
- Summarize what you read.
- Think of a title for the story
- Draw a picture that summarizes what you learned.
- The point of view of the lecture was_____.

Building Writing

Purpose: A technique that is more extensive than Kindling. Each step in the Building Writing process helps students to develop a coherent position.

Procedure: The Building Writing process begins with a question that invites students to generate ideas. After the students have generated their ideas, they compare their responses with another student, adding additional ideas to their list or expanding upon their existing ideas, thoughts, and feelings. After the discussion, the students shape their final response to the question. Their response is judged upon the following criteria: understanding of the content, ability to use the content to support their positions, and ability to write a clear and coherent paragraph/essay.

STEPS:

1. The teacher lays out question(s) for students to ponder.

2. The teacher invites students to generate initial ideas.

3. Students get more ideas from a partner.

4. Students hold discussions to clarify and extend their thinking.

5. Students think through final responses.

6. Students shape their final response in writing.

Building Writing Response Sheet

Question _____

Initial Response (20 pts)_____

_____

_____

Generating Ideas (15 pts)_____

_____

_____

Class Discussion (15 pts)

____ Participation   ____ Critical Thinking   ____ Content Mastery

Written Response (50 pts)

____ Understanding of content (15 pts)   ____ Use of content to support positions (15 pts)

____ Clarity and coherence (10 pts)   ____ Writing conventions (10 pts)

_____

_____

_____

_____

_____

_____

_____

_____

_____

_____

_____

_____

_____

_____

_____

_____

_____

_____

_____

_____

Collaborative Summarizing

Purpose: A group writing structure that teaches students how to create powerful summaries through collaboration and consensus negotiation.

Procedure: Collaborative Summarizing begins after students have read a text, heard a lecture, seen a film, or received some other form of input that the teacher wants them to summarize. The teacher instructs students to list, individually, the 3 - 6 most important ideas from the material they have learned. Students then pair up and review the rules for consensus negotiation:

1.   Avoid win-lose situations

2.   Avoid quick and simple solutions

3.   Make sure all positions use evidence and are logical.

   Using these guidelines, the partners create a negotiated list that reflects their combined agreement on the 3 - 6 most important ideas. Then, each student pair meets with another pair and the four students renegotiate their lists again and order the list so that it makes will makes sense as a summary. Once this ordered list is developed, each group of four prepares a collaborative summary.

   One of the most important aspects of Collaborative Summarizing is that it does not simply stop once the summary is created; rather it is designed to help students extract from their own work a general set of principles for creating summaries. After each group of four develops a summary, groups pair up again. Each group of four shares its summary with the other group and then, together, all eight students develop a set of criteria for powerful summaries. These criteria become the basis for students to use in writing summaries throughout the year.

STEPS:

1.   After students have received input (e.g., text, lecture, film, etc.), the teacher asks them to identify the 3 - 6 most important ideas.

2.   Students pair up and review the rules for consensus negotiation, which they use to negotiate and combine their lists.

3.   Student pairs match up and each group of four negotiates the list again to form a comprehensive and ordered list of the 3 - 6 most important ideas.

4.   These groups of four use their negotiated list to create a collaborative summary.

(c) 2001, The Thoughtful Education Press
(800) 962-4432

5. Each group of four shares and discusses its summary with another group of four.

6. These groups of eight create a set of criteria for powerful summaries.

7. Students use these criteria throughout the year to develop summaries on their own.

Example: *Collaborative Summary of a Reading on Hatshepsut, Egypt's only Female Pharaoh*

Topic: Hatshepsut, Female Pharaoh

My key ideas
(Student 1 generates list independently)

1. For 3000 years, all the other pharaohs were men.
2. Women could become priests, but never pharaohs.
3. She said she was the daughter of the god of wind and air.
4. Ships brought back lots of treasures and Egypt became richer.
5. She had many buildings built.

My partner's key ideas
(Student 2 generates list independently)

1. Hatshepsut was the only woman pharaoh.
2. When Thutmose II died, his son was too young to become pharaoh, so Hatshepsut took over.
3. Once she was pharaoh, she ordered a giant temple with huge statues of her to be built.
4. The ships she sent brought back elephant tusks, baboons, gold, and myrrh, which was used to make incense and medicine.
5. She ruled Egypt for over twenty years.

Our key ideas
(Students 1 and 2 negotiate their lists)

1. When Thutmose II died, his son was too young to become pharaoh, so Hatshepsut took over.
2. Hatshepsut was the only woman pharaoh to rule Egypt.
3. She had many buildings, temples, and public places built.
4. Hatshepsut was a good pharaoh.
5. She sent ships to East Africa, which brought back treasure and myrrh.

Continued on the next page

Final list
*(Groups of four create a comprehensive list and arrange it so that it
will make sense as a summary)*

1. Hatshepsut was the only woman pharaoh to rule Egypt.
2. When Thutmose II died, his son was too young to become pharaoh, so Hatshepsut took over.
3. Hatshepsut was a good pharaoh.
4. She had many buildings, temples, and public places built and repaired.
5. She sent ships to East Africa, which brought back treasure and myrrh and made Egypt richer and more beautiful.

Collaborative Summary
(Students use the final list to create summaries individually)

In the whole history of Egypt, only one woman ever became pharaoh. Her name was Hatshepsut. She was able to become pharaoh because when Thutmose II died, Thutmose III was too young to become a pharaoh. Hatshepsut was supposed to rule only until Thutmose III was old enough to be a pharaoh. But Hatshepsut also wanted to become the pharaoh, so she took over.

Hatshepsut was a good pharaoh. During her rule, she had many beautiful public places, buildings, and temples built. Old buildings and monuments were repaired. She sent many trading and exploring expeditions out, and the ships returned with treasure and myrrh. Egypt became richer and more beautiful while she was pharaoh.

Criteria for Powerful Summaries
*(Students return to their groups of four to read their work and determine
what makes for a quality summary)*

1. A powerful summary is accurate and thorough.
2. A powerful summary identifies main ideas and important details.
3. A powerful summary is clear and well organized.
4. A powerful summary correctly applies the rules of:
  -punctuation
  -grammar
  -spelling
  -capitalization.

Collaborative Summarizing Worksheet

Topic_____

My key ideas:

1._____
2._____
3._____
4._____
5._____
6._____

My partner's key ideas:

1._____
2._____
3._____
4._____
5._____
6._____

Our key ideas:

1._____
2._____
3._____
4._____
5._____
6._____

Their key ideas:

1._____
2._____
3._____
4._____
5._____
6._____

What we all agreed on:

1._____
2._____
3._____
4._____
5._____
6._____

Criteria for Powerful Summaries

1._____
2._____
3._____
4._____
5._____
6._____

4-2-1 Free Write

Purpose: A tool used to review previously taught material and for students to identify collaboratively the one big idea that holds the material together.

Procedure: Students are given a 4-2-1 Free Write organizer. Individually, each student identifies the four important ideas previously presented in the lesson, unit of study, or reading. Each student meets with another student to compare ideas and decide on the two most important from their lists of four. The pair then meets with another pair. The groups of four discuss their two ideas and together arrive at a consensus on the single most important idea. The teacher collects and records the big ideas from each group on the board, then selects one from the list. Students free write for five minutes, explaining all that they know about the big idea. After writing, the students return to their groups of four to read and review their free writes, followed by a whole-class discussion about how the big idea has shaped the unit, lesson, or reading.

STEPS:

1. Students study information learned in class.

2. Students record the four big ideas individually on their organizer.

3. Students meet in pairs to share their ideas and agree on the two most important ideas from their lists.

4. Student pairs meet with another pair, share their two ideas, and reach a consensus on which idea is the most important.

5. The teacher collects the most important ideas from each student group and records them on the board.

6. The teacher selects the one most important idea and asks each student to free write for 5 minutes. (Write without stopping; if students are stuck, they have to write about why they are stuck. The purpose is for students to explain what they know about the big idea so someone who was not in the class would understand it.)

7. Students return to their groups of four to listen to each other's written responses.

8. The teacher leads a discussion of the big idea.

4-2-1 Free Write Organizer

Individually: Four Ideas

**Pairs: Two
Central Ideas**

**Groups of Four:
The One Big Idea**

Free Write

Writer's Club

Purpose: A writing support group in which group members share and discuss their written work and generate feedback on how to improve it.

Procedure: Writing is a difficult process, and student writers need support in developing written products. The Writer's Club allows students to test their work in a non-judgmental atmosphere and receive feedback from their peers who are equally invested in this writing process. Once students have produced a written product, they meet in Writer's Clubs consisting of three to five students.

The Writer's Club can be set up in many different ways. Often, each member reads her piece and then receives feedback from the entire group based on specific criteria such as: use of powerful words and phrases, coherence of sentences, clarity of the writing, and writing mechanics. Different kinds of written products will call for different criteria (e.g., persuasive essays might focus on clarity of position, use of evidence, responsiveness to counterarguments). Another option is to provide Writer's Clubs with a menu of questions or activities designed to help each writer understand his piece more clearly. One member of the group might serve as the moderator who can choose questions or activities from the menu which the other members use to respond to the reader's piece. When the moderator reads her piece, another group member can moderate.

Whatever structure the teacher and students choose to create, it is important for group members to listen carefully to the reader and each other, and to provide constructive feedback. Each reader must also listen carefully to the group's responses without defending herself or her piece. The emphasis should be placed on helping each other to improve in the writing process.

STEPS:
---

1. After students have created a written product or a draft, they break up into Writer's Clubs (3 - 5 students).

2. All members of the Writer's Club read their piece aloud.

3. Members of the Writer's Club listen carefully and provide constructive feedback to each reader on how to improve the piece.

4. Each member of the group uses the feedback to revise and refine his written product.

Example: *Writer's Club Questions (To be Selected by the Moderator)*

Literal Questions

- Summarize the piece.

- Give the main points.

- Give a headline/title to this piece.

Personal Questions

- How did this piece affect you?

- What feelings did this piece arouse in you?

Rules of the Writer's Club

1. Everyone reads.

2. Listeners respond to questions chosen by the moderator.

3. Writer listens to responses and does not defend self or piece.

4. When moderator reads, someone else moderates.

Interpretive Questions

- What stood out for you?

- What's the most important part of this piece?

- If this piece were yours, how would you change it?

Creative Questions

- If this piece were a kind of:
  clothing,
  music,
  period of history,
  weather
  what would it be?

(c) 2001, The Thoughtful Education Press
(800) 962-4432

Tools For Improving Students' Vocabulary

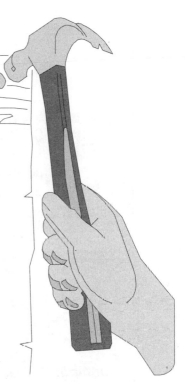

Visualizing Vocabulary

Purpose: A creative and visual way to enrich students' study of vocabulary.

Procedure: Students begin by defining the word they are studying. Then they find three or four pictures, or make an original drawing that illustrates the word. The students then explain why the pictures are good examples of the word.

STEPS:

1. Students define the word.

2. Students select or draw three or four pictures that represent the word.

3. Students write a sentence explaining why the pictures are good examples of the word.

Example: *Visualizing "Erudition"*

Erudition: Deep, extensive learning.

These four pictures are good examples of erudition because these are things that people with deep, extensive learning might have or do.

Deep Processing

Purpose: A tool that encourages students to explore important words deeply by using words, feelings, sensory information, and visualization.

Procedure: Some words are so central to a text or lesson (think of "friendship" when reading Arnold Lobel's *Frog and Toad* books with primary students, or "gravity" in a high-school physics classroom) that a simple rephrasing of the definition, followed by using the word in context, will not reveal its richness or importance. Deep Processing is a vocabulary tool that brings important words with layered meanings to life. The tool guides students to a deep and personally-meaningful understanding through multiple learning pathways: language, images, feelings, and physical sensations.

To use the Deep Processing tool, the teacher selects a word that is central to understanding the content. The teacher provides students with the word and asks them to generate some preliminary associations. Then, students explore the word using the Deep Processing framework. Afterwards, the teacher and students hold a discussion in which they share their insights and make connections between the Deep Processing session and the current text or lesson. Deep Processing is also an effective framework for remembering: By storing information in four different ways, the memory becomes stronger and easier to recall.

STEPS:

1. The teacher selects a word that is crucial to understanding the text or lesson.

2. Students generate preliminary associations for the word.

3. Students use the Deep Processing framework to explore the word through:
   - words
   - visualization
   - sensory information
   - feelings

4. The class discusses the Deep Processing session and makes connections to the text or lesson.

---

3.   Physical Understanding

Make a physical symbol with your body that explains what *devotion* means to you.

2.   Emotional Understanding

What are some of the feelings you have whon you are devoted to someone or something? What are the feelings you have when someone is devoted to you? Use colors to describe your feelings.

*T*hink about the word *devotion*. Are you devoted to someone or something? Is someone devoted to you?

4.   Linguistic
          Understanding

In your own words, write down what *devotion* means to you.

1. Visual Understanding

Create a picture in your mind of *devotion*. See yourself and the other person or thing. What does *devotion* look like? Draw a picture.

Deep Processing Organizer

Physical Understanding

Emotional Understanding

Linguistic Understanding

Visual Understanding

Vocabulary Notebook

Purpose: A tool for helping students use context clues to develop their own perspective on the meaning of difficult words. By asking students to assess their own understanding of a word and then to formulate a definition based on the context, Vocabulary Notebook builds reading independence. Then, by comparing their own definitions to the dictionary definitions and creating a visual representation for each word, students build a deep, long-lasting understanding of essential words. The notebook structure of the tool helps students keep yearlong track of their vocabulary development and facilitates review.

Procedure: Students read selected text, focusing especially on the difficult words. (Often, these words are pre-selected by the teacher and visually highlighted.) *Ultimately, the goal is to develop independence so that students can use this strategy on their own.* Students then mark each word in the text using the following symbols:

√ = I know this word

—— = I think I know this word (underline)

○ = I don't know this word (circle)

For each difficult word, students write their own definition. A definition is required for each word, including the words the student doesn't know. Students use semantic clues from the prefixes, suffixes, and root words as well as the context to help them formulate a preliminary definition.

Students next look up the words in a dictionary and record them, then compare the actual definitions with their own definitions by identifying similarities and differences between the definitions. Students select the meaning that is being used in the text. Finally, students complete processing activities to help them express and deepen their understanding of the words. To make meanings memorable, students classify and qualify the words, create an analogy and a visual representation (icon, symbol, sketch, etc.), and find synonyms for each word.

STEPS:

1. Students read text, focusing on difficult words. (Often, these words are highlighted by the teacher.)

2. Students mark each word using these symbols:
    √ = I know this word.
    ___ = I think I know this word (underline).
    o = I don't know this word (circle).

---

3. Using semantic and context clues, students write their own definition for each word.

4. Students look up dictionary definitions and record them. They then compare their own definition with the dictionary's.

5. Students complete processing activities to help them flesh out and deepen their understanding of the words.

Example: *Vocabulary Notebook for Martin Luther King Jr.'s "Letter from Birmingham Jail"*

Word	My Definition	Dictionary Definition	Comparison
legitimate	allowed	sanctioned by law or custom; lawful; conforming to or abiding by the law;	The sense of my definition was right, but not specific enough. The dictionary definition makes it clear that something legitimate is recognized by the law.
segregation	A time when African Americans used to have separate schools.	the policy or practice of forcing racial groups to live apart from each other	I thought of segregation more as a time period, but the dictionary calls it a practice or policy.
paradoxical	When something doesn't make sense.	adjective form of "paradox" A paradox is: a statement contrary to common belief; a statement that is self-contradictory	Again, I was close. My definition wasn't an adjective, though.
advocate	to want something to happen	to speak or write in support of	The dictionary is much more specific than I was. My definition was only about wanting something to happen, but when you advocate something, you go farther. You actually speak or write about your support.
statutes	laws	a formal rule; an established regulation; a law passed by a legislative body and set forth in a formal document	I was right on this one. Statutes and laws are practically synonyms.
unjust	unfair	unfair; contrary to justice	I was right on this one, too. Unjust and unfair are synonyms.

(c) 2001, The Thoughtful Education Press
(800) 962-4432

Example: *Processing Activity for "Unjust"*

Mastery
Critical Attributes

Class: Ethics

Qualifications: Deals with the relative fairness
of an action or law

Interpersonal
Synonyms
(Find a word that means the same or about the
same as . . .)

unfair
wrong
unethical
immoral

**Word:
unjust**

Understanding
**Create an Analogy Using One of the
Following Forms:** Degree of intensity, location,
opposites, specific to general, part to whole, or
tool and person

Unjust: Fair
as
Chaotic: Organized

Self-Expressive
Visualize the Word
(Pictures, icons, symbols, etc.,)

Tools for Mastering and Deepening Vocabulary

(Adapted from Davis and Dudley, 1994)

Purpose: A set of innovative and powerful vocabulary tools that help students internalize and contextualize new words and discover the deeper meanings that give words and ideas their force. It is one thing to recite a dictionary definition; it is quite another to understand how important ideas animate and enrich our thinking. By using strategies like contextualization, storytelling, comparison, characterization, and others, students learn to unlock the full potential of words and concepts.

Procedures/Variations:

Context

Contexts give shapes and shades to definitions. Students can explore the "relativity" of important words and ideas by examining them in various contexts.

Example:

Definitions place a concept in context. It's all in the what you call it! The name you give something can make all the difference. Take a car, for example. It can be a form of transportation, a type of vehicle, or a status symbol.

Notice how the context you choose is a powerful influence on the definition.

When a car is viewed as a form of transportation, its characteristics are:_____
_____

And it is compared with:_____

When a car is viewed as a status symbol, its characteristics are:_____
_____

And it is compared with:_____

Choose an idea to define in two different contexts:

When a_____ is viewed as a_____, its characteristics are:_____
_____

And it is compared with:_____

When a_____ is viewed as a_____, its characteristics are:_____
_____

And it is compared with:_____

                    (c) 2001, The Thoughtful Education Press
(800) 962-4432

Storytelling

Storytelling is a powerful way for students to define words and concepts. To use this tool, have students analyze common stories to determine what they define. Then ask students to choose a concept and create a story that defines the concept.

Example:

Sometimes the storyteller steals the show.

Do you remember the story of the little boy who cried wolf? The story is a powerful way to define trustworthiness. What about "The Lion and the Mouse," where the mouse rescued the lion by removing a thorn from his paw? When the lion reluctantly freed the mouse in return for a favor, he never expected to collect. The story defines the power of compassion.

What is your favorite story? What does it define?

Story:_____

_____

_____

_____

Defines:_____

_____

_____

_____

_____

Choose a concept you are studying and make up a story about it.

_____

_____

_____

_____

_____

_____

_____

_____

_____

_____

Examples and Non-examples

Everyone knows how examples clarify definitions. But what is often overlooked is that non-examples double this clarity by serving as an opposing idea that brings the critical attributes of a word or idea into sharp focus.

Example:

What does it mean to you for someone to be fun? Give some examples of things a person would do that would make you think he or she was "fun."

_____

_____

_____

What is the opposite of fun? What are some examples of things a person would do that would take them out of the category of fun?

_____

_____

_____

Think about what it adds to have the "non-fun" examples.

_____

_____

_____

Write your definition of "fun" based on the examples and non-examples you gave.

_____

_____

_____

Try defining one of the concepts you are studying in this way. If you can't name non-examples, you probably don't have full grasp of the concept yet.

Examples:_____

_____

_____

Non-examples:_____

_____

_____

Analogies

Analogies help students to see words and their meanings in different lights by making the familiar strange or the strange familiar. Ask students to stretch their understanding by creating and explaining analogies.

Example:

We all have teachers we love and those that drive us crazy. Think about some of the teachers you have had and pick a word from the list below to describe each one.

friend	dictator	coach	cheerleader
scientist	lawyer	band leader	taskmaster
timekeeper	facilitator	leader	supporter
judge	resource	president	gang leader

Teacher Similes

Example: Mr. Nicandri is like a coach because he tries to develop your thinking muscles in science.

_____

_____

_____

_____

Similes like these will make us smile, or frown, or shake our heads. But they all make us look at teachers a little bit differently. Pick one teacher and explain the simile in more detail, using examples.

_____

_____

_____

_____

Try using a simile or an analogy to define a concept or person you are studying.

Comparison

Like analogies, comparisons help students to extract deeper meaning from words and concepts by comparing them to other words and concepts. Comparisons go even further by asking students to consider how the two terms are not only alike, but also different.

Example:

Are cars, trains, and buses equal? In one sense they are: They're all transportation. Are bananas, oranges, and kiwis equal? They're all fruits, but different in size, shape, and taste. The category something belongs to tells us something about it. Comparing it to other members of the same category also tells us something.

Think about what a comparison of fruit tells you. How are a kiwi and an apple alike?

_____

_____

_____

How are they different?

_____

_____

_____

Define a kiwi by comparing it with an apple.

_____

_____

_____

Define an apple by comparing it with a kiwi.

_____

_____

_____

This strategy works especially well when one of the concepts is familiar and the other one is strange. Try it on a concept you are studying.

(c) 2001, The Thoughtful Education Press
(800) 962-4432

Characteristics

A definition describes the key characteristics of a word; however, most terms have far more characteristics than a basic dictionary definition can provide. Think of how many characteristics you can generate for the word "hamburger" for example, and then go look "hamburger" up in the dictionary. Missing from the dictionary will be dozens of characteristics regarding smell, taste, where you buy them, what types there are, etc. Help students build the character of important words and concepts by using many characteristics to create a definition.

Example:

The more characteristics you use when you define a concept, the more character you give it. Just like a person, character makes a concept easy to recognize and understand.

You can build character in many different ways. Try it with the concept of "trees."

What you see_____

What you hear_____

What you smell_____

What it feels like_____

What it does_____

Where it is_____

What kind it is_____

Where it came from_____

What it is used for_____

Why it is valued_____

Types of it_____

How it grows_____

Use these characteristics to write a definition. Try this on a concept you are studying.

_____

_____

_____

_____

_____

_____

_____

_____

(c) 2001, The Thoughtful Education Press
(800) 962-4432

Etymologies

Like people, words have histories. Often, the origins of words and they way their meanings have shifted over time makes for fascinating study. Allow students to explore the histories of words. Ask them to explain how the original meaning is still intact or has changed over time.

Example:

Where do words come from?

Look at some of these origins:

        absent - *from the Latin, to be away*

        blunt - *from Middle English, blind*

        dollar - *from Low German, five shillings*

        mousse - *from French, moss or froth*

        pride - *from Old Norse, bravery*

        serene - *from Latin, clear, unclouded sky*

        thing - *from Old Norse, a meeting or assembly*

What do you notice about the etymologies?_____

_____

_____

_____

Find out the origins of five words you use. See if you can trace today's meaning back to the original meaning. Be a detective and look for clues about why and how the words changed.

Word:_____   Word:_____

Today's meaning:_____   Today's meaning:_____

Origin:_____   Origin:_____

Word:_____   Word:_____

Today's meaning:_____   Today's meaning:_____

Origin:_____   Origin:_____

        Word:_____

        Today's meaning:_____

        Origin:_____

Tools for Practicing Vocabulary

(Adapted from Benevento, 1997)

Purpose: A set of tried-and-true vocabulary tools that help students learn, remember, and use vocabulary words. There are many ways to help students practice vocabulary, and many teachers have their favorite vocabulary activities. These tools together form a Vocabulary Toolkit, which both teachers and students can use to teach and learn new words.

Procedures/Variations:

Multiple Meanings

Students read pairs of sentences. From a provided word bank, they choose a word that fits in both sentences. They then find a sentence from the chapter that uses the word and write it below the pair of sentences. Students explain which use of the word is most like the sentence in the book.

Example:

---

1.   All of our papers were (uniform) in size and shape.
2.   The sailor's (uniform) consisted of a navy blue shirt, bell bottom pants, and a white tie.

Sentence from Chapter 1:

_____

_____

The meaning of the word in Chapter 1 is most like sentence number_____ because

_____ .

Three's A Crowd!

Students examine three words. They decide which one doesn't belong and explain why.

Example:

	Which word doesn't belong?	Why?
intelligence, courage, aptitude		
tribute, honor, rituals		

All's Well that Ends Well!

This technique focuses on suffixes and how they alter a word's meaning. Students examine words, then write the root word and the suffix. They write a new word by adding a different ending to the root word, and they define the new word. Often students refer to a list or table that outlines the types of suffixes and their meanings.

Example:

Word	Root	Ending	New Word	Meaning
hesitation	hesitate	tion	hesitated	paused in acting or deciding

Synonyms and Antonyms

For both synonym and antonym activities, students examine sentences with specific words underlined. Students examine the sentence and the underlined word and then provide a synonym or antonym for the word. Often, the words students use are contained in a word bank from which students can select. It is always a good idea for teachers to ask students to explain their choices.

Context Clues

Students find different words used in the text. (Students can be given a list of difficult words, or the words can be underlined, or the students can identify these words themselves.) They write a definition based on the context, then compare their definition with a dictionary definition.

Glossaries

From their vocabulary words, students create specialized glossaries (e.g., words about war, words that express emotions, etc.).

Crossword Puzzles

Students create crossword puzzles from their vocabulary words by creating definition-based clues. Students try to solve each other's puzzles.

Categories

The teacher provides a category or attribute (e.g., words that describe, action verbs, words relating to government). Students select words from their vocabulary lists that fit each category. This game can be played in teams, individually, and in a written or oral format.

Vocabulary Bingo

The teacher makes grids with enough space to write definitions in each box. As words are called out, students place markers in the corresponding boxes. The first student with a column, row, or diagonal wins.

Vocabulary Riddles

Students create riddles for their vocabulary words.

Vocabulary Songs

Students write raps, jingles, ballads, blues, etc. about what they've read or learned using vocabulary words in the lyrics.

Analogies

Students develop and explain analogies using vocabulary words.

Tools For
Building Students'
Memory Skills

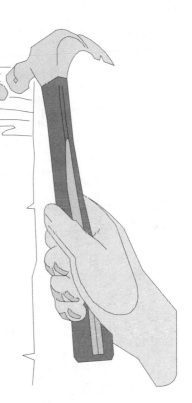

Memory Frameworks

Purpose: A set of techniques used to help students memorize information. When using Memory Frameworks, students should mass practice at the beginning and distribute it over time.

Procedures/Variations:

Rhyming Pegword

A memory framework which uses ten "slots" that rhyme with the numbers one through ten:

1 is a bun	6 is a pile of sticks
2 is a shoe	7 is heaven
3 is a tree	8 is a gate
4 is a door	9 is a line
5 is a hive	10 is a hen

The students first identify the information they wish to remember. They then organize the information into a list. Finally, they deposit the information in the slots.

Example: *Remembering the Basic Principles of the Constitution*

1. We the People/All power is a gift of the people.
2. Popular sovereignty/Not monarchy.
3. Limited government can only use powers given by the people.
4. Cannot make up new laws.
5. Some powers government cannot have, e.g., limiting free speech.
6. Federalism/Balance between state and local power.
7. Separation of powers.
8. Legislative branch makes laws.
9. Executive branch enforces laws.
10. Judiciary branch rules on validity of laws.

The student would try to form an image of the first idea, *We the People/All power a gift of the people*, with the peg word "bun." The student might imagine buns wrapped up with ribbons being given as a gift from a group of people to a government official. The student would then try to connect the second idea, *Popular sovereignty/Not monarchy,* to a shoe. The student could imagine plain shoes of people standing on a picture of a monarch with a "No" symbol on it. The student would continue the process until she has slotted all of the information and then would practice retrieving the information randomly.

(c) 2001, The Thoughtful Education Press
(800) 962-4432

Familiar Place

The Familiar Place Framework is an easy framework to create. The student imagines a familiar place and then mentally moves around the place, identifying familiar objects in the order in which they appear in the place. For example, if a student uses her kitchen, she might first select the door or entryway, then moving to the right, her kitchen table, then the kitchen chairs, refrigerator, stove, sink, etc. Each object represents a slot with which to associate a bit of information. A variation of the Familiar Place Framework is to imagine a route one commonly takes.

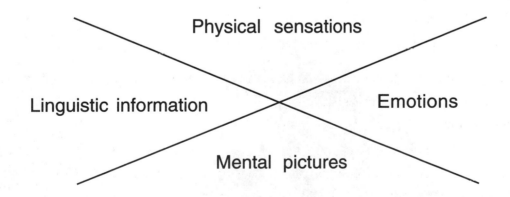

Visualizing

Visualizing is another technique to facilitate memory. Techniques like Mind's Eye, Etch a Sketch, Sketch to Stretch, and Visualizing Vocabulary are good examples of visual tools theta build deep memories. Visualizing can also be used to connect an absurd association or familiar image with the new information to be remembered. For example, students were challenged to learn the names of the bones in the human body. For the more difficult names, they created absurd mental pictures such as two pals driving a car (metacarpals); radial tires (radius); and a skull-shaped flower pot of geraniums (cranium).

Deep Processing

A memory has components that are visual, physical, emotional, and verbal. If we were to draw a diagram of a thought, we would see overlapping interrelationships among these components:

Physical sensations

Linguistic information   Emotions

Mental pictures

Deep Processing uses these four components as a memory framework to help students highlight important information, retrieve information easily, and stimulate creative thinking. Students are asked to first remember something by developing vivid mental pictures. They then explain the picture in words, talking to themselves as they do and listening to their own words. Next, students identify their personal feelings/emotions in relation to the memory. Finally, students use physical information (touch, taste, sight, smell, sound) associated with the memory to develop even deeper associations.

For example, students compare two descriptions of Paul Revere's ride by deciding which is more memorable:

Description 1:
Paul Revere rode through the town warning the colonists of the British army's invasion.

or

Description 2:
Through the blustering night the Old Church Bell rang Dong, Dong, Dong. . . Paul Revere heard the twelve chimes and knew his time was running out. Before the clock would chime again, the British would be there to hear the dong from the Old Church Bell.

And so, as the last Dong's echo fell from the night, the sound of pounding horse's hooves could be heard as Paul Revere's horse swept him through the town. As he rode, Paul Revere sounded the warning, "The British are coming! The British are coming! Prepare to fight. The British are coming!"

Students then experience and describe the passage in pictures, words, physical sensations, and inner feelings. Finally, students recall a personal experience using all four elements.

Mnemonics

Purpose: A set of tools used to remember and retrieve information. While rote repetition has been the primary method taught for memorizing, there has been renewed interest and development of techniques known as mnemonics for helping students master and retain information. With each of these techniques, students should rehearse regularly, massing their practice at the beginning and then distributing it over time.

Procedures/Variations:

Organizing

The more information is organized, the easier it is to learn and retain. In using this technique, the students group and label information according to similar elements so that it is easier to learn and remember. For example, in trying to remember the outline of pre-Civil War history, the students might organize information according to the major regions: North, South, and West.

Ordering

Information is easier to remember if it is learned in a series, especially if there is meaning to the series. For example, if we wish to have the students learn the names of the digestive organs, it will be easier if the students start from the mouth and trace the food through the long intestines.

Acronyms

Acronyms are letters used to make up a code word. Each letter represents a specific idea the student needs to remember. The acronym serves as an organizer and chunks the ideas. For example, if the teacher wanted her students to remember the four basic principles of memory (connect, organize, deep process, and elaborate) she might present them using the acronym C.O.D.E. Acronyms can be used by the teacher to present information or by the student to review the information.

Memory sentences

Memory sentences, like acronyms, help students to organize and chunk information. For example, in mathematics, students are taught the order of operations through the sentence "Please excuse my dear Aunt Sally," which stands for *parentheses, exponents, multiply, divide, add, subtract.*

Tools For Deepening Student Reflection

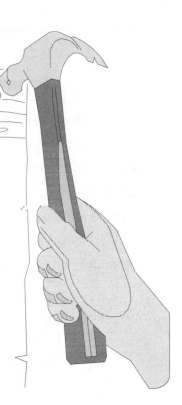

1.2.3.4.

Purpose: A tool used to encourage students to reflect actively upon a lesson.

Procedure: The teacher stops five minutes before the end of the lesson and has students reflect upon what was presented by writing in this format:

> 1 - Stands for the big idea.
>
> 2 - Stands for important details.
>
> 3 - Stands for personal connections.
>
> 4 - Stands for questions students have about the content.

After the students have completed their reflections, they can share them with a neighbor or small group, or the teacher can call on students to share them with the entire class. The teacher can also collect the responses to obtain feedback from the class on the lesson. Another option has the teacher preparing his/her own 1.2.3.4. prior to the lesson, and then comparing student responses against the instructional goals and his/her own 1.2.3.4. The 1.2.3.4. technique is a wonderful way to keep students active for the last five minutes of a class, when many of them have packed up their bags and their minds. It also stimulates conversation about the class: As students move from one class period to another they often converse with their friends about what they wrote.

STEPS:

1. Five minutes before the end of the lesson students stop to reflect.

2. The teacher explains what *1.2.3.4.* means:

   1=Big idea presented today in class
   2=Important details you want to remember
   3=Personal connections you made between the content and your
      life outside of school
   4=Questions you have about the content

3. Students record responses in Learning Logs.

---

4.   Students may share in pairs, small groups, or with the whole class.

5.   The teacher collects responses and compares student reactions with his/her own conceptions of the big ideas and important details.

6.   The teacher uses questions for review for the next day.

Note: 1.2.3.4. can also be used at the beginning of a lesson to review prior to presenting new content. To use this tool at the beginning of the lesson, substitute the following steps for 4, 5, and 6 above:

4.   Students read and research to collect information, verifying what they know, clarifying misunderstandings, finding answers to questions generated.

5.   Students then communicate their new understanding using a web, visualization, organizer, written summary, etc.

6.   The teacher connects students' new understanding with the lesson to be taught.

Reflective Writing

Purpose: A technique that provides students with an opportunity to reflect upon what they have been learning.

Procedure: The teacher first provides students with information via a lecture, movie, presentation, field trip, reading assignment, or discussion. After a number of key ideas have been presented, the input stops and the students are asked to reflect on what they have been learning in their Learning Logs.

When students have responded, the teacher has students share their thoughts in small groups. The teacher then leads a discussion with the entire class. After the class discussion, the teacher continues with the presentation of the new information. The cycle can repeat as necessary. Students are invited to discuss their logs each day in order to review the content, clarify their confusion, and raise questions about their homework or yesterday's lesson.

STEPS:

1. Information is provided to the students.

2. Class stops after a number of key ideas have been presented.

3. The teacher frames reflective questions for students to ponder.

4. Students organize thoughts.

5. Students record ideas.

6. Students match thoughts with other students' ideas.

7. Students summarize and synthesize.

Examples: *Reflective Writing Questions for All Occasions*

In the beginning of the lesson:
- *Write three important points you remember from yesterday's lesson.*
- *What questions do you have from yesterday's lesson?*
- *What do you predict we will discuss today in class?*

(c) 2001, The Thoughtful Education Press
(800) 962-4432

At the end of the lesson:

- *What did you learn today?*
- *What surprised you?*
- *Today was like . . .*
- *The three most important ideas are . . .*

On the group process:

- *I helped move my group's thinking forward today because . . .*
- *The group helped my thinking because . . .*
- *One feeling I have about my participation today is . . .*
- *An example of how our group worked effectively today was . . .*

Example: *Sample Reflective Writing Format*

Topic _____   Date_____

Essential question(s) addressed:

_____

_____

_____

Key idea(s) presented:

_____

_____

_____

Connections I can make with other ideas:

_____

_____

_____

Questions I still have:

_____

_____

_____

Reflective Statements

Purpose: A technique that encourages students to reflect on a lesson, unit, or day's learning by completing one of four types of sentence stems: I learned . . ., I wonder . . ., I appreciate . . ., I now truly understand . . .

Procedure: At the end of a lesson or unit, the teacher invites students to reflect on what they have learned by completing one of these sentence stems:

> I learned...
> I wonder...
> I appreciate...
> I now truly understand...

Students record their thoughts in their Learning Logs and share their responses with the class. This provides both the teacher and the students with a quick assessment of both the cognitive and affective understanding of the class and helps in charting direction for instruction. (Often, responses to the "I wonder" stems help set up future inquiries into the topic.) An alternative way to use Reflective Statements is to have students respond to all four stems.

STEPS:

1. The teacher provides students with the four stems.

2. Students reflect upon their learning and complete one (or all four) of the stems.

3. Students record their ideas in their Learning Logs.

4. Students share their ideas with the class and together, the teacher and students develop a quick cognitive and affective assessment of the class's learning.

Reflecting in Style

Purpose: A tool that helps students reflect deeply on an assignment, homework, project, or specific content material. The tool asks students to reflect using various metacognitive approaches: literal restatement, logical analysis, creative thinking, and personal reaction.

Procedure: When students engage in thoughtful reflection, their understanding of both their work and themselves improves dramatically. Reflecting in Style encourages students to look back on their work and their thinking processes in four different ways, or "styles":

1. *Mastery-style reflection:* students restate what they have learned or what procedures they followed to complete their work.

2. *Understanding-style reflection:* students analyze their learning and their work, looking for signs of growth or questions they still have.

3. *Self-expressive-style reflection:* students look back on their work or learning creatively by exploring connections to other learning and by brainstorming ways to improve the process next time.

4. *Interpersonal-style reflection:* students use their personal reactions, values, and spontaneous impressions to investigate how their learning affected them.

To implement Reflecting in Style, the teacher explains and models the four styles of reflection for students. Once students understand the various approaches to looking back on their learning, the teacher provides them with questions and prompts in each of the four styles. When students have completed an assignment or learning experience, they use the teacher's questions and prompts to reflect in all four styles. Student reflection can become the basis for teacher-student conferences or whole-class discussions on essential content, students' working habits, and the learning process in general.

STEPS:

1. The teacher explains the four styles of reflection and models each with students.

2. After an assignment or learning experience, the teacher provides questions and prompts in all four styles.

3. Students use these prompts to reflect on their learning or work in all four styles.

---

4.   The teacher and students follow up through conferences or discussions on content, work habits, and the learning process.

Examples: *Reflecting on Homework, Portfolio Assignments, Characters, and Projects*

Reflecting on My Homework

Mastery-Style Reflection
What did I do to get my homework done?

What steps did I follow? Where did I do it? When did I do it?

Interpersonal-Style Reflection
How am I feeling about getting my homework done?

Understanding-Style Reflection
What did I do to make sure the homework was done well?
Did I do my homework the way I had planned? How did it work? Did anything occur that caused me to do my homework differently from what I had planned? If so, what and how did it work?

Self-Expressive-Style Reflection
What am I learning about getting homework done so that I can feel good about it and know that I've done a good job?
Is there anything I need to consider or change in doing my homework in the future?

Reflecting on a Project

Mastery-Style Reflection
What did you do to complete the project? Describe the steps you took.

Interpersonal-Style Reflection
What did you like about doing this project? What didn't you like? How has carrying out this project changed the way you view yourself as a learner?

Understanding-Style Reflection
Which steps worked best for you? Why do you think so? As you did the project, what didn't work so well for you? How do you know you did a good job? How do you know the project was done well? List at least three reasons.

Self-Expressive-Style Reflection
In doing this project, what did you learn that you might apply in doing another project?
If you were to do this project again, what might you do differently?

Reflecting on a Portfolio Assignment
Title of the assignment:_____

Mastery Reflection
What did I do to complete the assignment?

Describe what I did, how I did it, when I did it, and whom I did it with.

Interpersonal Reflection
How do I feel about this piece of work?

Understanding Reflection
How does this work show my progress?

Comparing this work with similar work I've done in the past, what progress am I making?

Self-Expressive Reflection
Taking into account my thinking, what am I learning about myself as a learner?

Reflecting on a Character in a Story

Mastery-Style Reflection
Who is the character?

What's his/her name?

What are some of his/her characteristics?

Interpersonal-Style Reflection
What do you like about__
_____?

What don't you like about
_____?

If you were this character, what would you have done?

Understanding-Style Reflection
Which characteristics are most important for this person to exhibit? Why do you think so?

How important is the character to the story?

Self-Expressive-Style Reflection
How might the story be different if this character were not in the story?

How might this character fit in another story that you have read?

Tools for Classroom Questioning

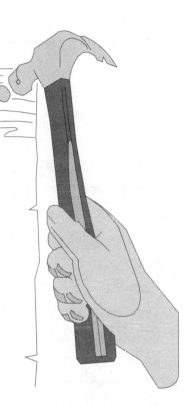

Questing

Purpose: This tool, adapted from the work of Strong, Hanson, and Silver (1995) is used to improve the quality and depth of student answers to questions. Questing is built upon the belief in the *cooperative* nature of questions and the *provisional* nature of questions.

Questing emphasizes the cooperative nature of asking questions and finding answers rather than the hierarchical nature of question and answer, since it is a process in which students and teacher work together to explore and search for answers. Questing also emphasizes the provisional nature of all answers. Every answer is only the first step on the road to a more satisfactory answer, a building block out of which students can construct better and more meaningful answers through careful use of feedback and further questions.

Procedures: The first step in Questing is to pose a question to all students, making sure that students have access to the information they need to respond to the question and that they understand the thinking required to answer the question. Every question is an invitation to think, but different questions require different kinds of thinking. It is important for the teacher to analyze the type of thinking she is asking students to engage in and to model the thinking before the question is asked. The next step is to establish a gap between the asking and answering. The teacher should discourage students from answering too quickly or impulsively; only when the thought process is slowed down can real thinking take place. The next step is to invite students to search for answers in notes or pictures. Only the simplest questions have answers that are readily at hand--thoughtful questions require searching. Have students jot down notes or sketches of their answers. This will help them make implicit responses explicit and clarify their thinking. The final step is to have students talk in small groups. This will provide students with an opportunity to test their ideas and maximize participation. The teacher is then ready to lead a discussion with the class.

STEPS:

1. The teacher questions all the students.

2. The teacher and students understand and model the thinking. Also, the teacher provides access to the information students will need to respond to the question.

3. The teacher establishes a gap between the asking and answering. Students should stop and think.

---

4.   Students search for answers in notes and pictures. They should write, draw, jot down, or scribble their responses so that they can see their thinking and clarify their ideas.

5.   The class talks in small groups to allow students to test their thinking, communicate their ideas, and participate in the questioning process. Then the whole class engages in a discussion of the question.

Example: *Questing in a High-School Biology Class*

1.	**Q**uestion all students	1.	*How is a cell like a city?*
2.	**U**nderstand and model	2.	*To create a direct analogy, list everything you know about the two ideas you are comparing and then identify commonalities. Look for unusual and insightful connections.*
3.	**E**stablish a gap between asking and answering.	3.	*List what you know about cells and cities. Now look for interesting connections between the two concepts.*
4.	**S**earch for answers in notes and pictures.	4.	*Jot down your ideas in your Write to Learn book.*
5.	**T**alk in small groups.	5.	*Share your ideas with a neighbor. Put a check mark next to those ideas which are similar. See if you can generate two new connections.*

Q-SPACE

Purpose: This set of behaviors, adapted from the work of Strong, Hanson, and Silver (1995), is used when responding to students' answers and will increase the depth of students' thought.

Procedure: The way in which teachers receive and respond to students' answers plays an important role in determining the depth and type of thinking that follows. Once a student has responded to a question, the teacher can do one of three things: withhold response, ask further questions, or make a statement. By consciously weaving these options together, the teacher can create a Questing-Space (Q-SPACE) that can be used to deepen and strengthen student thinking. Q-SPACE consists of the following components:

── COMPONENTS: ──

Question: The quest is a journey or exploration of content initiated by the posing of a focus question.

Silence and wait time: Students need time to think prior to responding, while responding, and following a response. The teacher should wait at least 5 seconds and maintain eye contact before responding. Depending on the type of questions and the thinking required, up to 15 seconds of wait time may be appropriate.

Probing: Responding to an answer with another question or request forces students to explain or support their response and will expose as much of the students' thinking as possible.

- *What evidence do you have to support that idea?*
- *Explain how you came to that conclusion.*
- *What do you mean by_____?*

Accepting: Accepting all answers without judging them is important. If answers are considered provisional, then all answers have the potential for being acceptable. Provisional acceptance of thinking and of communicating the thinking is important.

- *I see.*
- *That's possible.*
- *Let me record your ideas.*

Clarifying and correcting: Take action by paraphrasing a student's response. Clarifying helps students to hear, understand, and reflect upon their own thinking.

- *What I hear you saying . . .*
- *Can someone else restate what John has said?*

Elaborating and extending: Ask students to expand on an idea. Where probing looks for reasons behind a particular answer, elaborating looks to where the answer might lead. It can also encourage students to make generalizations that unite and explain a variety of data.

- *Can you give another example?*
- *What conclusions can you draw from this?*

Response Techniques

Purpose: A variety of techniques used to vary the approach to calling on students and to promote participation in classroom activities.

Procedure: There are many ways to call upon students in class. The important thing is for the teacher to vary the techniques. One obvious technique is to call on the students who have their *hands raised*. In *random calling* the teacher poses a question and then randomly calls on students in the class to respond. Alternatively, the teacher can design a deck of cards with the students' names and choose one card at a time. In *student calling* students who are called upon can call on other students to respond. In a *whip* the teacher goes around the classroom, obtaining a short response to the question from everyone.

STEPS:

1. The teacher poses a question.

2. The teacher gives students time to think and construct a response, then calls on a student.

3. The teacher uses a variety of techniques: Raised Hand, Random Calling, Student Calling, Whip.

Examples:

Raised Hands: The teacher calls on students who raise their hands.

Random Calling: The teacher calls on students randomly. The teacher may use name cards that are shuffled randomly or pull names out of a hat.

Student Calling: The teacher invites a student to call upon another student he would like to hear from.

Whip: The teacher calls on a row or table, asking each member to share an idea. The teacher can use a whip to move a question around an entire room.

What's My Question?

Purpose: A tool for generating questions about a topic by asking students to speculate on what questions the teacher might ask.

Procedure: The teacher shows a book cover, poster, or picture to the students and asks students to speculate on what possible questions she might ask about the text. Students then generate a variety of questions. The teacher selects some of the student questions and asks students to generate possible responses. Later, when students read the text, they compare their responses with the text.

STEPS:

1. Students examine the cover of a book or title of a text (or relevant picture, poster, etc.).

2. Students generate a list of possible questions they think the teacher might ask about the text.

3. The teacher selects some of the questions and has students generate possible responses.

4. The students then read the text to compare it with their initial responses.

Example: *What's My Question for a Book Cover on the Dust Bowl*

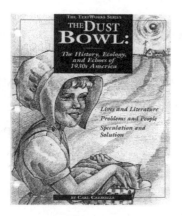

Why is it called The Dust Bowl?
What things/beliefs were important to the people in the Dust Bowl?
How were the these people like us?
How were they different?
What hardships did they face?
What is their legacy?
What if we were lived during the Dust Bowl? What would we see and do?

Questions in Style

Purpose: A questioning framework that fosters in students the "Four R's" of critical thinking: recalling, reasoning, reorganizing/applying, and relating personally. By developing a repertoire of questioning techniques (or "styles"), teachers help students to explore and expose the layers of information that make up any content.

Procedure: True understanding is multifaceted. In order to understand a topic fully, we need to be able to gather various types of information. This is accomplished by asking questions. For example, if we wanted to understand the endangerment of the Asian tiger, we would need to ask:

Mastery questions, which help us to recall and gather the facts of the situation. (Where do tigers live? What do they eat? How much land do they need to survive?)

Understanding questions, which help us to interpret patterns and draw logical conclusions. (What are the causes of endangerment? What are the effects? What lessons can we learn from other cases?)

Self-Expressive questions, which help us to speculate and apply solutions. (What would happen ecologically if the tiger became extinct? What are the possible solutions to this problem? What are the potential deterrents and how might they be overcome?)

Interpersonal questions, which help us to connect personal values and feelings to the topic. (Why should we fight to save the tigers? How are they important to people and to the world? What would it feel like to be endangered?)

These four types of questions correspond to what learning specialists call "learning styles" (Silver, Hanson, 1998, Morris, McCarthy, 1999). A simple and powerful way to help both teachers and students understand these four styles quickly is to think of them as the "Four R's of learning: recalling (Mastery questions), reasoning (Understanding questions), reorganizing/applying (Self-Expressive questions), and relating personally (Interpersonal questions). The goal, over time, is to help students gain independence in using these four types of questions in order to explore the multiple layers of meaning in the content they are studying.

1. The teacher models with students the four styles of questions and the "Four R's" of critical thinking.

2. Using the Question Stem Menu (see below), the teacher develops and asks all four styles of questions throughout the year.

3. Before answering, students review the question and determine what style of thinking it requires.

4. Students recall or gather the information needed to construct a response.

5. Students reflect on the styles of questions and their preferences for each type.

6. As students develop confidence in answering style-based questions, the teacher fosters their independence by encouraging them to ask and answer their own style-based questions.

Mastery questions ask students to:

Recall facts:
• Who? What? Where? When? How?

Supply information based on observation:
• What did you observe?
• Can you describe it?

Sequence and proceduralize:
• Develop a timeline.
• What are the steps?

Interpersonal questions ask students to:

Empathize and describe feelings:
• How would you feel if _____ happened to you? How do you think _____ felt?
• What decision would you make?

Value and appreciate:
• Why is _____ important to you?
• What's the value of _____?

Explore human-interest problems:
• How would you advise or console _____?
• How would you help each side come to an agreement?

Understanding questions ask students to:

Make connections:
• What are the similarities and differences?
• What are the causes/effects?

Interpret and infer:
• Why? Can you explain it?
• Can you prove it using evidence?

Explore underlying meanings:
• What are the hidden assumptions?
• What does your discovery prove?

Self-Expressive questions ask students to:

Explain metaphorically or symbolically:
• How is _____ like _____?
• Develop a metaphor for _____.

Develop images, hypotheses, and predictions:
• What would happen if _____?
• Can you imagine _____? What would it look like/be like?
• What do you think will happen next? Why?

Develop original products:
• Create a poem, icon, skit, or sculpture to represent _____.

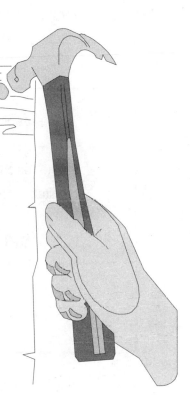

Tools for
Teaching and
Practicing Skills

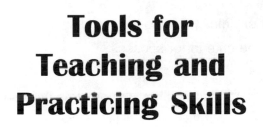

Think Aloud

Purpose: A tool used by teachers to model the thinking processes students will be engaged in while completing a particular task.

Process: The teacher introduces the task to the students, explains what the final product will look like, and establishes the criteria for success. The teacher then demonstrates how to complete the task while modeling the thinking involved out loud to students. Once the Think Aloud is complete, the teacher checks to make sure students understand what they have to do to accomplish the task successfully.

STEPS:

1. The teacher introduces the task to students.

2. The teacher explains what the final product should look like and establishes the criteria for success.

3. The teacher demonstrates how to complete the task while modeling the thinking out loud.

4. Students and teacher check for understanding.

Example: *Think Aloud on How to Write A Chapter Summary*

Task and Criteria: *We are going to write a chapter summary. Here is an example of a chapter summary. It explains the big ideas and the important details concisely, in the writer's own words, using appropriate writing conventions.*

Think Aloud: *I am going to do a Think Aloud while I show you how one goes about writing a summary. First, I read the page. Then I ask myself: What are the key words? When I identify the key words, I see how they're connected and look for a main idea. Once I've got the main idea, I write it as a sentence and then select two or three important details that support the main idea. I then write it as a paragraph. I read it over to see if it makes sense and check my spelling and punctuation. That's how I develop a good summary.*

Check for Understanding: *Are there any questions?*

Four-Phase Practice

Purpose: A practice structure that maximizes the learning and teaching potential of skill acquisition.

Procedure: Four-Phase Practice helps students internalize and master essential skills by breaking practice into four interrelated phases:

The first phase in Four-Phase Practice is *modeling.* In this phase, the teacher establishes the steps in the skill and delivers a demonstration of what the learner needs to do in order to successfully implement the skill. It is important that the instructor explains and demonstrates precisely what is expected of the students. As the teacher models the steps in the skill, he or she should also model the correct thinking process relative to the skill. To do this effectively, the teacher should "think out loud." (See Think Aloud, pg. 130.)

The second phase is known as *directed practice*, during which the teacher checks that students understand what was modeled. Using specific and focused questions, the teacher leads students through the skill. Some appropriate questions would be: "What do you do first?" or, "Why do we do this?" These questions remind students of the key steps in the skill. They also help the teacher evaluate students' progress and level of understanding.

The next phase is *guided practice*. Guided practice is used to clarify the skill as well as to build greater independence in performing the skill. The teacher should assign a few highly-focused exercises or tasks. Additionally, the teacher should monitor the student's of the group's performance; provide support and corrective feedback; make himself/herself available for students who need help; and look for patterns in student errors. Students, for their part, have the responsibility of performing the task. They must also ask questions and seek help as needed, for the responsibility has now been shifted onto them and away from the teacher.

The final phase of Four-Phase Practice is *independent practice*. Now, students must work on their own to practice and refine the skill without direct teacher supervision. Students are responsible for making decisions about how to do the work, the order in which the task will be completed, the material and equipment they will need, and how the task will be evaluated.

STEPS:

1. The teacher models the skill for students while exposing the relevant thinking processes by thinking aloud.

2. The teacher directs students through a few examples by asking specific questions about each step in the skill.

(c) 2001, The Thoughtful Education Press
(800) 962-4432

3. The teacher provides a selection of examples for students to work through on their own while students generate the questions themselves. (The teacher circulates and observes student practice.)

4. The teacher assigns independent practice examples and asks students to monitor their strengths and weaknesses.

Example: *Using Four-Phase Practice to Teach Students How to Solve Analogies (SAT Preparation)*

Modeling: The teacher begins by solving five analogies on an overhead projector. As she solves the analogies, she shows students the thinking process involved by thinking out loud:

1. Read the relationship and comprehend the words.

2. If you do not comprehend a word or words, try to approximate the definition using vocabulary cues (e.g., prefixes, suffixes, roots, similarities to words you do know).

3. Convert the capitalized words into a clear sentence that describes their relationship.

4. Compare the relationship to the relationship in the answer pairs.

5. Eliminate all answers that don't fit the relationship.

6. If you can't eliminate all the answers, refine your sentence so that the relationship is more specific and explicit.

7. Select the answer that best fits the relationship.

The teacher and students then complete one example together to help students internalize the process.

Directed Practice: In Phase 2, the teacher leads students through five examples. As the class works through the examples, the teacher directs their attention to each step in the process by asking questions like: *What do we do first? What happens if we can't eliminate all but one of the answers?*

Guided Practice: At this point, students assume greater responsibility by working on practice examples independently. Students ask themselves the questions needed to solve each analogy. During this time, the teacher walks around the room to monitor student progress and to provide help and feedback as needed.

Independent Practice: The teacher asks students to take a sample analogy test on their own and to assess and report back on their performance.

Tools For Reviewing

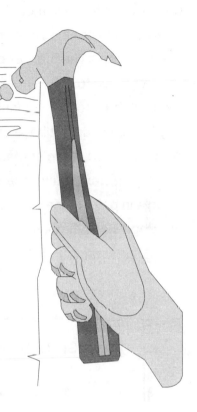

Boggle

Purpose: A fun and effective tool to help students rehearse and remember information for a test, quiz, or other form of assessment.

Procedure: After the teacher has presented material to be learned, time is provided for students to review their notes. Students must pay attention to the big ideas and important details of the lesson. The students are then asked to put their notes aside and, on a piece of paper, retrieve all of the information they can. The teacher can guide the student retrieval by providing categories.

After two to five minutes, the students are asked to put their pens and pencils down and to join a group of three to four students to share their lists. It is important to inform students that they should add any idea they do not have on their own list because they will need it to compete with other students in the next round of the strategy. The teacher should remind them that no idea is too big or small.

In the next round, the students leave their team to Boggle with other students. Students can Boggle in pairs or triads. Students get a point for every idea they have on their list that the person they are Boggling with does not have. The students then return to their teams and total their points.

After scoring the Boggle play, the teacher leads a review of the items that earned the students points.

STEPS:

1. Students review notes from previously presented material for 2 minutes.

2. Students retrieve and write down as many big ideas and important details as they can remember in 2 to 5 minutes.

3. Students take 2 minutes to rehearse with 3 or 4 other students. Students share their lists and add any ideas that they don't have.

4. Students pair up for 2 minutes. They rack up points using the Boggle technique. They earn a point for every idea they have that their Boggle partner doesn't have.

5. Students return to their team and compute the team's score.

6. The teacher leads a review of the material and identifies what is important to know and understand for tomorrow's test or assessment.

---

7.   The teacher collects team scores and rewards effort according to team rank, a fixed standard, or community chest.

Example: *Look over your notes on cell division. Close your notebook and write everything you remember about cell division for 2 minutes. Next, join a study group and add all the new ideas to your list. Now, we're ready to Boggle!*

Teacher's Notes:

1.   Encourage students to generate big ideas and important details.

2.   Provide categories, if necessary, for students to generate and organize their information.

3.   Remind students to add to their list when sharing with their team because they will need to use their lists to Boggle in the next round.

4.   Remember when Boggling, students get points for what is on their list and not on their opponent's; therefore, it is important for students to have the basic information everyone should know to protect themselves and also to seek information other students might not know.

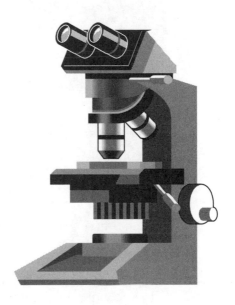

Reproducible

Boggle Gamesheet

Information Retrieval

Group Rehearsal

Missed Information

TOTAL POINTS: **Earned** [ ]   **Missed** [ ]

Tools for Promoting Active, In-depth Learning   136   (c) 2001, The Thoughtful Education Press
(800) 962-4432

Panel Discussion

Purpose: A tool used to engage students in the content being learned by asking questions and involving them in meaningful discussion.

Procedure: Students are asked to write down on a card a question they have about the material being studied in class. A panel of four to six students is selected and seated in front of the class. The cards are collected and shuffled. Each panel member selects a card, reads it silently, and thinks of a response. The first panel member then reads his card out loud and gives a response. After the response is given, other panel members are asked to add to the initial member's response. This is continued until all panel members have contributed to the answer. The teacher rotates panel members frequently so that every student gets a chance to participate. A variation of the panel discussion is to have the audience pose the questions to the panel, or to ask panel members follow-up questions to their initial responses.

STEPS:

1. Students write down a question they have about the material being studied.

2. The teacher selects four to six students to participate in a panel discussion.

3. The cards are collected and shuffled. Each member of the panel selects a question to be discussed.

4. Panel members read the question silently and consider a response.

5. The first panel member reads his/her question aloud and responds.

6. Other panel members add to the initial response.

7. Members of the panel are rotated frequently so that all students get an opportunity to be panel members.

Categories

Purpose: A technique for forming groups and reviewing content.

Procedure: The teacher identifies a general theme or topic and categories according to the number of groups she wants to establish. The teacher then generates specific items for each category depending upon the number of students in each group. For example, if the subject is geography, specific categories could be land forms, weather, natural disasters, continents, countries, rivers, and mountain chains. The items for each category for a class of 28 students might be as follows:

Land forms	Weather	Disasters	Continents
island	humidity	tornado	Asia
peninsula	temperature	hurricane	Africa
isthmus	precipitation	earthquake	North America
plateau	wind	monsoon	Australia

Rivers	Mountain Ranges	Countries
Amazon	Rockies	United States
Nile	Urals	England
Mississippi	Pyrenees	China
Thames	Sierra Madre	South Africa

Each student is given a card with a specific term on it. The student is asked to identify the topic, then to consider the category in which the term belongs. The student then searches for others who fit into the same category. When most of the groups have found their members, the teacher brings the students to a halt and has those groups that are complete name their category, read their items, and explain why the items relate. The remaining students who have not found a group are coached by the others until they find their respective groups. At some point, the teacher may provide an answer key to help the students identify their groups.

A variation of this technique is to provide students with a single line from a limerick or other poetic form, such as a sonnet, which the students would have to reconstruct into a complete poem. Similarly, students can solve a mathematical equation and find others who have a similar answer. This technique is highly adaptable to various classroom needs.

STEPS:

1. The teacher chooses a topic, then formulates categories and specific items for each category depending on the number of groups and students in each group. Each item is placed on a card and distributed, one to each student.

2. Students mingle and try to find other students that they believe belong to their category.

3. Play stops when most students have come together.

4. Each group identifies its items and explains why the terms go together.

5. The remaining students are coached until they find their groups.

Examples: *Possible Categories*

- •Characters in literature
- •Television programs
- •Historical events or documents
- •Types of food
- •Parts of speech
- •Verb conjugations (e.g., preterite, past perfect, future, subjunctive, etc.)
- •Biological species
- •Elements from the periodic table

3-2-1

Purpose: A tool that provides a structure to help students develop a summary quickly.

Procedure: The teacher assigns a reading lesson, shows a video, or presents information to be learned. At the end of the lesson, the teacher asks the students to write three new facts, two questions, and one big idea to turn into the teacher. The 3-2-1 may be written on an index card or slip of paper. At the end of a class period, the students may be told that the 3-2-1 will be their exit card from the class. This summary may be used at any point in the lesson when the teacher wants students to think about their learning in order to provide feedback.

STEPS:

1. The teacher provides input (lecture, reading, film, lesson, etc.)

2. The students are asked to write about:
    Three things "That really interest me" (Facts)
    Two things "I'd like to know more about" (Questions)
    One "Big idea from today" (Theme or large concept)

3. The teacher uses the summaries to direct instruction or provide feedback.

Variation: *Using 3-2-1 to Meet Your Needs*

The stems attached to the 3-2-1 can be changed to fit the lesson, the content, and the students.

For example, when studying a famous person or major character in a book, you might use this format:
    Three most important events in this person's life
    Two questions you would ask this person if you
        could talk with him/her
    One way in which you are like this person

Mastery Review

Purpose: A tool used to involve all students in reviewing essential content and to correct misunderstandings about content.

Procedure: Students are first given the opportunity to study information they have covered in class. Since the brain learns better when information is placed in a context, the teacher then orally reviews the content in a story format, emphasizing what is essential for students to know and understand. Within the story, the teacher periodically frames questions for the students to answer. The students record their responses on paper. While the students are responding, the teacher writes the answer on the board or overhead for the students to use as a check to determine if their responses are correct. The teacher then continues the process of developing the story while increasing the level of difficulty of the questions. At the conclusion of the review, the teacher asks the students to discuss how well they did, to reflect on what they know and understand, and to decide what they need to work on to improve their understanding.

STEPS:

1. Students study information learned in class.

2. The teacher narrates a content story and periodically asks a question to the class.

3. Students respond to the question in writing.

4. The teacher records the answer to the question on the board while the students are writing their responses.

5. Students review the answer and check and correct if necessary.

6. The teacher invites the students to reflect on their understanding of the questions.

7. The teacher and students discuss what they know, understand, and have to work on.

Example: *Mastery Review for a Test on Cells* (Questions appear in **bold**, answers in *italics*)

SUBJECT: Biology
TOPIC: Cells

As we began our study of **living things, which are better known as** _____ *(organ-isms)*, we discussed the characteristics that distinguish that which is living, or once living, from that which was never alive. We were able to develop a list of several characteristics. As we looked over our list we noticed that it included such items as the ability to reproduce, to grow, to develop, and to use energy. However, one characteristic was different than the others and did not describe a process. **What was that characteristic?** *(Living things are made of basic units of structure called cells.)* This characteristic was one of the last defined by scientists. **What invention allowed this characteristic to be added to the list? And who was its inventor?** *(the microscope, Anton von Leeuwenhoek)*

Once the discovery of cells was made and as microscopes became more and more sophisticated, scientists began to learn more about this incredible building block of organisms. One of the first structures discovered was the outermost boundary of the cell that selectively controls what enters and leaves. **What is this boundary called and what word is used to describe its selective property?** *(cell membrane, semi-permeable)* **Draw and label it.** As we move into the cell, we find that there are many structures within the cell, each with its own special design and function. **What term is used to describe these parts?** *(organelles)* The organelles of the cell are suspended in a material that fills the cell. **What is this gelatinous material called?** *(cytoplasm)*

As we begin our journey through the cell, the first major organelle that we come upon is the nucleus. **Draw and label it. What is its function?** *(controls all cell activities)* But wait! What's this? Something appears to be wrong with our cell! It does not seem able to provide useful energy for its activities! **What organelle is missing?** *(mitochondria)* **Add the mitochondria to your drawing and label it.**

The cell is often compared to a factory. **If this is true, what structures would represent the storage areas, packaging plants, transportation centers, and garbage disposal areas? Draw and label them**. *(vacuoles, Golgi bodies, endoplasmic reticulum (ER), and lysosomes)*

As we leave the cell and look back at it, with all of its organelles, we realize that it is not just the basic unit of structure of all living organisms but it is also the basic unit of function as well. **Explain why this statement is true.** *(All of the functions that are carried out at a cellular level are carried out in a grander scale at the organism level.)*

Outburst

Purpose: A fun way to review important content information.

Procedure: In order to play Outburst, the teacher breaks students up into groups of three to five students. (There should be an even number of groups.) Half of the groups will be Group 1s, while the other half will be Group 2s.

The teacher provides four fact-generating categories to all Group 1s and four different fact-generating categories to all Group 2s. (For example, fact-generating categories for a unit on Ancient Egypt might be: *famous rulers, advantages provided by the Nile River, medical inventions, technological inventions, Egyptian gods, invaders, famous monuments, roles in society.*) To play, students write down at least five facts for each category on an index card.

Once the cards have been completed, the competition can begin. Each Group 1 should read the category on the top of one of the four game cards just completed and allow Group 2 two minutes to shout out as many facts as its members are able to generate. For each item that is shouted out that matches an item written on Group 1's card, Group 2 will receive a point. If Group 2 gets all of the facts on Group 1's card, Group 2 will receive an additional bonus of three points. Group 1 will need to keep track of answers by checking items on the card as they are shouted out by Group 2. After two minutes have expired, Group 1 should review the items to clarify what was said and what was not.

Group 1 then continues play until all four of its cards have been completed. Play then switches, and Group 1 becomes the playing team as Group 2 reads the categories on its cards and allows Group 1 two minutes to generate answers for each. The team with the most points at the end of the competition is the winner of Outburst.

STEPS:

1. The teacher breaks the class up into an even number of groups (3 to 5 members). Half of the groups will be group 1s, while the other half will be group 2s.

2. The teacher provides four different fact-generating categories to each group. A fact-generating category is one whose items are facts that can be verified as fitting or not fitting the category (e.g., prime numbers, Romantic poets, amphibians, wartime presidents.)

3. Students in each group write down at least five facts for each of the four

---

(c) 2001, The Thoughtful Education Press
(800) 962-4432

provided categories.

4.   Group 1 reads the category on one completed game card and allows Group 2 two minutes to shout out as many facts as its members can generate. For each shouted item that matches an item on Group 1's card, Group 2 receives a point. If Group 2 gets all of the facts on the card, Group 2 gets three additional points.

5.   Group 1 keeps track of Group 2's answers by checking off items on the card. After two minutes have elapsed, Group 1 reviews the items to clarify what Group 2 said and missed. Play continues for cards 2, 3, and 4.

6.   Groups 1 and 2 switch roles: Group 2 reads the categories while Group 1 shouts out the answers.

7.   The group with the most points at the end of the competition wins.

Example: *Outburst Categories for a Unit on the Age of Exploration*

Group 1	Group 2
1. Names of explorers	1. Places explored
2. Results of exploration	2. Important figures (excluding explorers)
3. Reasons for exploration	3. New technology
4. Facts about life at sea	4. Problems/hardships faced by explorers

Tools for Helping Students Present Ideas

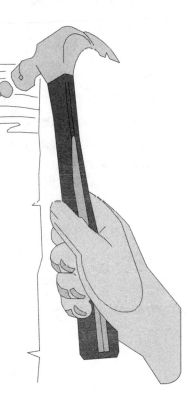

Poster Session

Purpose: A novel way for students to present and exchange ideas about a topic being discussed or studied.

Procedure: Students select a concept or idea related to the topic or unit being studied. They then prepare a visual display of the concept on a poster board. The poster can include words and pictures, and should be self-explanatory. That is, observers should easily understand the idea without any further written or oral explanation. Often, criteria for evaluation of posters include clarity, comprehensiveness, color, and creativity. Students can work alone or in pairs. They can also be asked to write a small narrative to support their visualization. Students post their visuals around the room and then circulate freely, viewing and discussing others' drawings. The teacher may give students adhesive notes to record and provide feedback to other students about their work. The class then convenes and the teacher leads a discussion about the work (what students learned and what they found most valuable). Posters can also be used for students to describe their thoughts and feelings about a topic.

STEPS:

1. Students select a concept or idea to be visualized on poster board. Students can use words or pictures. Posters must be self-explanatory. (Criteria for evaluating posters are: Is it clear? Is it comprehensive? Is it colorful? Is it creative?)

2. Students post their visuals around the room and circulate freely, viewing and discussing.

3. Class convenes to discuss ideas.

4. The teacher continues lesson, building on student responses.

Example: *In your group, prepare a poster that represents your understanding of democracy.*

Group-to-Group Teaching

Purpose: A technique for assigning different work to different groups. Each group completes the assignment, then creates a lesson to teach what group members have learned to the rest of the class.

Procedure: The teacher selects a topic that involves different ideas, events, positions, concepts, or approaches. The topic should be one that encourages an exchange of positions or information. The class is then divided into groups of four or five. Each group is responsible for completing the given assignment. Groups are given time to prepare a presentation for the other groups. A spokesperson is selected from each group to address the class. After a brief presentation, the class members are encouraged to ask questions of the presenter or to offer their own views. The other members of the spokesperson's group are also invited to join in the discussion. Each group is given an opportunity to make a presentation and to respond to audience questions and comments. After the presentations, the teacher leads a discussion with the class that integrates each group's contributions.

STEPS:

1. The teacher selects a topic that can be broken into parts.

2. The class breaks into small groups of four to five students. Each group is assigned a segment to study.

3. Each group prepares a class presentation.

4. Each group selects a spokesperson to present the group's ideas.

5. Students ask questions and share their own perspective on the issue being discussed.

6. After each group has made a presentation, the teacher leads the class in a discussion, comparing and contrasting the ideas of each group.

Examples: *A Potpourri of Topics for Group-to-Group Teaching*

Different writers' perspectives   Different forms of energy

Different historical points of view   Different computer software

Different short stories   Different environmental problems

        (c) 2001, The Thoughtful Education Press
(800) 962-4432

Graphic Organizers

Purpose: Tools to help students visualize, prioritize, organize, and present information.

Procedure: A graphic organizer is a mental map that illustrates how information is organized. It helps students to see information as a set of relationships rather than isolated facts. Once information and relationships are recorded on a graphic organizer, students can then use the organizer to interpret, evaluate, and draw conclusions about the information.

Graphic organizers are multidimensional learning tools serving many purposes. They can help students organize ideas in preparing essays, reports, or oral presentations. Students can use organizers to prepare displays and demonstrations, to collect and organize information, and to improve their memorization skills. Teachers can use organizers to illustrate and explain relationships found in textual material. They can use organizers to prepare effective lectures and demonstrations and to design bulletin boards, murals, or multimedia presentations. Teachers can also use organizers to demonstrate specific thinking skills and to assist visual learners in perceiving abstract concepts.

Examples: *Common Types of Graphic Organizers*

Topic Organizer

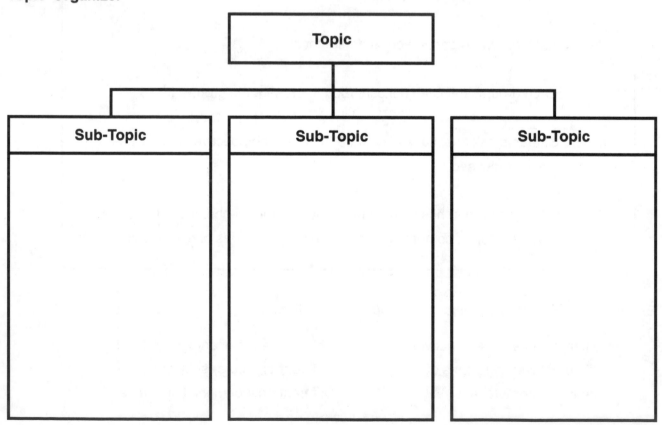

Process Organizer

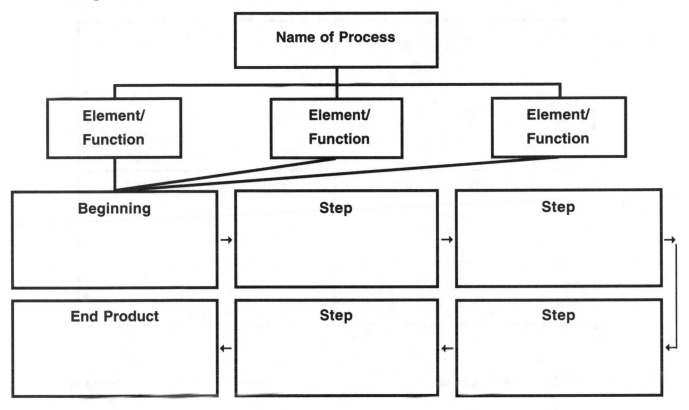

Cycle Organizer

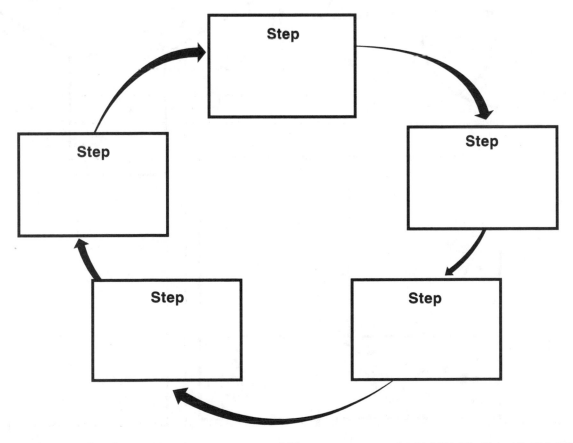

Design Organizer

Structure	Purpose
Arguments For/Against	**Variations & Alterations**

Compare and Contrast Organizers

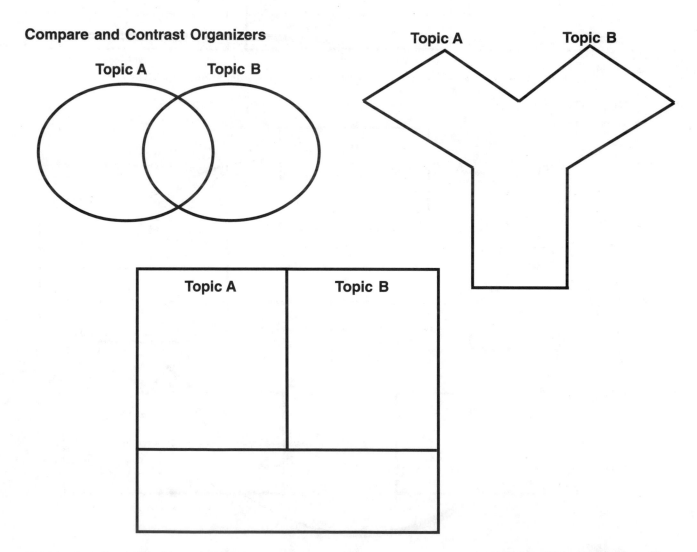

Topic A   Topic B

Topic A   Topic B

Topic A	Topic B

Generalization Organizer

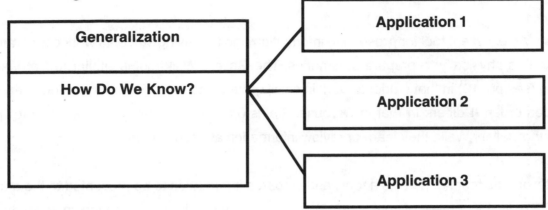

Generalization
How Do We Know?

Application 1

Application 2

Application 3

Descriptive Organizer

Item	Criteria

Ranking Organizers

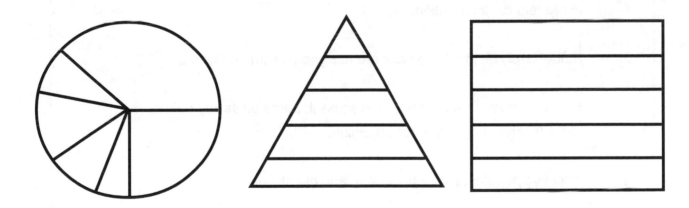

Interval Organizers

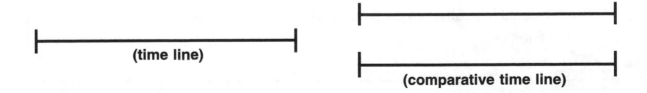

(time line)

(comparative time line)

Gallery Walk

Purpose: An excellent tool for presenting information and for having students work cooperatively and move around physically to prepare summaries. The Gallery Walk tool is similar to Carousel Brainstorming (see pg. 19) in that students work in small groups and move from one station to another in a prescribed order. It differs in that in Carousel Brainstorming, students generate ideas to questions while in the Gallery Walk, they learn or review information at each station.

Procedure: The teacher selects a topic and prepares information to be presented to the students by having them visit a number of stations (5-8) around the room. The students work in small groups (2-4 per team), review the information at the station, discuss it, record it on an organizer, and decide what they believe are the important points to be learned. A variety of material can be used at each station, including readings, charts, videos, slides, newspapers, objects, experiments, etc. After the students are finished visiting each station, they look over their notes and generate a team summary, which can include words, demonstrations, pictures, and visual aids. The students then present their summaries and reflect upon their work as a group and on the process of preparing a summary.

STEPS:

1. The teacher selects the content to be presented.

2. The teacher divides the content into 5 to 8 stations, using a variety of methods to present the information.

3. Students divide into teams and are assigned a starting station.

4. Students review the information, discuss it, agree on its key points, and record their ideas on a group organizer.

5. After five minutes, students move to another station.

6. After completing the cycle, students present a group summary using words, pictures, demonstrations, charts, etc., as needed.

7. The students reflect on the group work and on what makes a summary powerful.

(c) 2001, The Thoughtful Education Press
(800) 962-4432

Examples: *Three Teachers' Gallery Walks*

A science teacher used the Gallery Walk to introduce her students to the topics they would be studying throughout the semester. At each station she used pictures and words related to her 7 major topics: the scientific method, ecosystems, biospheres, adaptation, weather, environmental issues, and technology. The students visited each station, interpreted the information the teacher provided, and then presented what they believed was a summary of the content and questions to be addressed during the year.

A social studies teacher used the Gallery Walk to teach about the Roaring 20's. At one station he had newspaper headlines from the time period. At another station he had two editorials about women's right to vote. At a third station he had graphs that showed statistics related to the growth of the automobile industry between 1920 to 1925. A fourth station had reading selections from the *Great Gatsby*. Another station had comparative pictures of women from the turn of the century and pictures of women from the Roaring 20's. The last two stations had the 18th Amendment declaring prohibition and two video clips from the movie, *The Roaring 20's*. After the students visited all of the stations, they prepared a group summary of the material, focused on why the 20's were called the Roaring 20's.

An art teacher used the Gallery Walk to introduce his students to Monet's style. Around the room he hung eight pictures representing various periods and themes in Monet's work. Students walked around the room, analyzing and taking notes on each painting. For their summary task, students had to decide on the six most important elements in Monet's style and explain the reasoning behind their choices.

Reproducible

Gallery Walk Planning Form

Topic_____

What do I want my students to:

Know? (Facts, details, skills)	Understand? (Big ideas, concepts, issues, controversies)	Appreciate and value? (Perspectives, cultural and human contributions, interdisciplinary connections)

Stations:

Title_____ Material:	Title_____ Material:
Title_____ Material:	Title_____ Material:
Title_____ Material:	Title_____ Material:
Title_____ Material:	Title_____ Material:

Tools for Checking Understanding

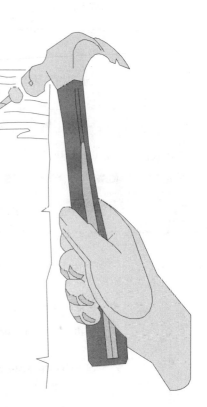

Explaining Solutions

Purpose: A tool that shows students how to convert their mathematical solutions into clearly-articulated explanations. Learning the skill of mathematical explanation is especially important because many state tests now require students to write down the steps they used to solve each math problem.

Procedure: Explaining Solutions works especially well with word problems. The teacher begins by selecting a problem from a current unit of study. Students read the problem carefully and underline what the problem is asking and the relevant information before solving the problem. After solving the problem, students reflect on the process and list, in chronological order, the steps they followed in developing a solution. Working with the teacher in the beginning, students convert the sequence of steps into a paragraph using transitional words and phrases, such as *first, next, then*, and *finally*. Students reread their explanations to determine if all the steps are included and chronological, if any terms need clarification, and if the chosen transitional words make the piece as understandable to the reader as possible. Students revise their explanations accordingly.

STEPS:

1. The teacher selects a word problem from the current unit.

2. Students read the problem carefully, underlining the question and the information needed to develop a solution.

3. Students solve the problem.

4. Students reflect on the process and list, in chronological order, the steps they followed.

5. With the teacher's help, students use transitional words to convert their steps into a paragraph. (Over time, students become independent.)

6. Students reread their explanations and ask:
   - Are all the steps included?
   - Are the steps in order?
   - Do any terms need to be clarified?
   - Are the transitional words well-chosen?

7. Students revise their explanations if necessary.

Surveying

Purpose: A tool to assess what students are thinking and to invite them to participate in class.

Procedure: The teacher asks the class a question which requires students to make a choice (e.g., *How many agree with this idea? How many disagree?*) Students can raise their hands, do thumbs up or down, etc., to show their responses. Both the teacher and the students get a quick sense of the class's ideas or feelings about the issue being discussed. The teacher can then use the students' responses to give direction to the lesson.

STEPS:

1. The teacher asks questions.

2. All students are invited to respond.

3. The teacher and students observe student responses.

4. The teacher continues the lesson, building on student responses.

Examples:

How many people agree with the answer?

How many people disagree?

How many people have ever felt so strongly about something that they were willing to protest?

(c) 2001, The Thoughtful Education Press
(800) 962-4432

Jeopardy

Purpose: A tool to stimulate creative thinking and to assess what students know and understand about a topic.

Procedure: The first step for the teacher is to introduce the topic being studied. Then the teacher asks, "If _____ is the answer, what are the questions?" The students generate as many questions as they can for which the given term would be the answer. The teacher records the possible questions. The questions are examined and grouped, and the teacher and class assess what they know and understand.

STEPS:

1. The teacher introduces a topic and reviews the structure of Jeopardy (students are given the answer and must generate the question).

2. The teacher asks, "If_____is the answer, what are the possible questions?"

3. Students generate responses.

4. The teacher collects and records students' responses.

5. Questions are examined and grouped in order to assess student knowledge and understanding.

Examples:

If quadratic equation is the answer, what are the possible questions?

If balance of power is the answer, what are the possible questions?

If Macbeth is the answer, what are the possible questions?

What? So What? Now What?

Purpose: A tool used to encourage students to reflect on an experience they have had in order to explore its implications.

Procedure: After a learning experience such as a game, simulation, role-play, debate, etc., the teacher asks students to share *WHAT* happened to them during the experience (What did they observe, notice, or what feelings or thoughts did they have during the experience?). The teacher then asks the students to ask themselves, *SO WHAT?* (What did they learn from the experience? What are the implications of the activity? Or, how did the experience relate to the real world?). Finally, the teacher asks students to consider, *NOW WHAT?* (How can the learning be extended or applied to other situations?).

STEPS:

1. The teacher provides an experience for students to participate in (simulation, role-playing, debate, etc.)

2. After the experience, the teacher asks students to reflect upon *WHAT* happened to them during the experience.

3. Next, the teacher asks the students to ask themselves, *SO WHAT?* and to reflect upon the learning from the experience.

4. Finally, the teacher asks the students to ask themselves, *NOW WHAT?* by considering ways to extend the learning to other situations.

What? So What? Now What? Student Form

What?_____
_____
_____
_____
_____
_____
_____

So What?_____
_____
_____
_____
_____
_____
_____

Now What?_____
_____
_____
_____
_____
_____

Feedback Tools

Purpose: A technique to obtain immediate feedback from students so that they can get appropriate help where and when it is most needed.

Procedure: The teacher designs a special code or system that allows the students to make it known when they do and do not understand. The code can be red light, yellow light, or green light cards (signifying extreme confusion, moderate confusion, and no confusion, respectively); hand signals; pictures; knowledge barometers; etc. The teacher begins teaching and periodically asks students to assess their understanding and provide him with feedback. If students say they are confused (red light cards, for example) the teacher asks students to state at what point they became confused and asks another student to restate what has been said. The teacher then reteaches the confusing material, slowing down or accelerating the pace of the presentation according to student feedback.

STEPS:

1. The teacher provides student with a code to give feedback on the lesson.

2. The teacher begins teaching, stopping periodically to allow students to offer feedback.

3. The teacher inquires about student confusion.

4. The teacher then reteaches the confusing material. Additional feed back can help the teacher determine whether to slow down or accelerate the pace of instruction.

Example: *Sample Picture Cards for Feedback Tools*

Got It

Slow Down

Confused

Comprehension Menus

Purpose: A tool used to assess the depth of student comprehension by asking students to recall facts, analyze big ideas, apply knowledge, and develop a personal perspective on key content.

Procedure: Much like Questions in Style (see pg. 126), Comprehension Menus ask students to think in all four learning styles. In the case of Comprehension Menus, students use the four styles to show what they know as follows:

In the *Mastery style*, students demonstrate their recall of facts and details.	In the *Interpersonal style*, students connect their learning to their own experiences, values, and feelings.
In the *Understanding style*, students focus on the overall meaning and the big ideas.	In the *Self-Expressive style*, students apply knowledge and use their imaginations.

Comprehension Menus provide teachers with a complete set of assessment information: from students' responses, teachers can see where students need to further develop their understanding of content and their thinking skills in general.

To use a Comprehension Menu in the classroom, the teacher creates at least four questions about the text or topic, one in each style (for help, see the Question Stem Menu on pg. 128). Students examine the questions, discuss the kind of thinking required to construct an answer, and then respond to each question. Often, students meet with other students to discuss and refine their responses. Once students have completed the menu, they reflect on the styles of the questions and their comfort level in each. Gradually, students should become independent in this process, creating and answering style-based questions to assess their own understanding of a text or topic.

STEPS:

1. The teacher creates at least four questions about a text or topic, one in each learning style. (For a list of question stems, see the Question Stem Menu on pg.)

2. Students examine each question to determine the kind of thinking it requires.

3. Students respond to each question.

4. Students reflect on and discuss how comfortable they are working in each style.

5. Over time, the teacher shifts responsibility to students by encouraging them to assess their own understanding of texts or topics.

Examples:

Fifth-Grade Comprehension Menu for Chapter 1 of My Brother Sam is Dead

Mastery Comprehension	Interpersonal Comprehension
• What is the setting for the story? Describe it. • Who are the four main characters and what are their traits?	• Which character do you relate to the most: Mr. Meeker, Sam, Tim, or Mrs. Meeker? • With whom do you agree, Sam or his father?
Understanding Comprehension	**Self-Expressive Comprehension**
• Why are the characters arguing? • What does Sam mean when he claims that some things are worth dying for?	• What do you imagine Tim is thinking during this argument? • How is a colony like a child?

High-School Comprehension Menu for Robert Frost's "The Road Not Taken"

Mastery Comprehension	Interpersonal Comprehension
• What is happening in the poem? • Who is speaking? • Identify the rhyme scheme.	• Do you relate to this poem? • Describe a "road less traveled by" from your own life (a decision where you chose the less popular or more difficult option).
Understanding Comprehension	**Self-Expressive Comprehension**
• What is the meaning of the poem? • What is meant by "And that has made all the difference?"	• What do you imagine Robert Frost was thinking when he wrote this? • How is a decision like a fork in the road?

(c) 2001, The Thoughtful Education Press
(800) 962-4432

Tools for Assessing Student Performances

(c) 2001, The Thoughtful Education Press
(800) 962-4432

Rubrics

Purpose: The quintessential tools for assessing student work. Rubrics provide clear descriptions of what achievement looks like at various levels.

Procedure: Rubrics are not simply grading devices for teachers, they are powerful learning tools that help students plan, produce, and revise their work. By reviewing the rubric with students before they begin working, the teacher helps students to understand what high-quality work looks like. Students then use this rubric all through the assessment process to measure the progress of their work and to seek ways to make it exemplary.

The rubric also provides an excellent foundation for student-teacher dialog about individual performance and for teacher feedback, which should be focused on how the students improve their work. There are two types of rubrics: analytic rubrics and holistic rubrics.

Analytic rubrics provide a separate line for each of the assessment criteria. For instance:

Task Description: *Students in Haverville Middle School math classes are asked to solve one non-routine math problem each week. From these, they select their best at the end of each month for inclusion in their Math Problem-Solving Portfolio. Each non-routine problem includes a restatement of the problem in the students' own words, the work they performed to solve the problem, and an explanation of their problem-solving process.*

Analytic Rubric for this Task

Problem Restatement	Work and Answer	Explanation of Problem Solving Process
Your problem statement clearly an accurately describes the problem in your own words.	Your work is complete and employs appropriate strategies; your answer is correct and properly labeled.	Your explanation is thorough, you explained how your worked, and gave reasons for all of your decisions.
Your problem statement is clear and accurate, but not in your own words.	Your work is fairly complete and employs effective strategies, but your answer is incorrect or improperly labeled.	Your explanation is fairly complete, but you skipped one or more key steps, or failed to provide reasons for your decisions.
Your problem statement is somewhat confused and/or inaccurate. It does not adequately describe the goal of your problem.	Your work is sketchy and incomplete, or you've employed inappropriate strategies and your answer is incorrect or unlabeled.	Your explanation is brief, absent, or unclear. You failed to provide good reasons for the decisions you made.

Holistic rubrics clump criteria together and group them by levels of achievement. For example:

Task Description: *Students in Duncan High School are asked to study the parts of a living cell, their functions, and the processes they use to fulfill their functions. They must then select an appropriate metaphor or analogy for a cell and its parts and describe, in visual and written form, how the parts of the cell correspond to the parts of the object they have selected as a metaphor.*

Holistic Rubric for This Task

Honors	Your metaphor is appropriate. You clearly describe the connections between all of the parts of the cell and the parts of your metaphor. In all cases, the connections you described were appropriate and worked through at a high level of detail for both structure and function. Your language is vivid, your ideas intriguing, and your paper well organized. Your visuals were clear, attractive, and original.
Proficient	Your metaphor is was well chosen. You described connections between most of the parts of the cell and the parts of your metaphor, but you may not have worked through these connections at a high level of detail for both structure and function. Your language is clear and your paper well organized. Your visuals were clear and attractive.
Apprentice	Your metaphor was adequate, but did not permit you to work through the connections between the parts of the cell and the parts of your metaphor due to insufficient detail. Your language is fairly clear, but your piece is not well organized. Your visuals are sketchy or incomplete.
Novice	Your metaphor is inappropriate or you have failed to use it to make important connections between the cell parts and your metaphor. The connections you do make are vague and lack detail. Your language and the overall structure of your piece are confused and lack organization. Your visuals are sketchy or absent.

STEPS:

1. The teacher reviews the rubric with students before they begin work on the task.

2. Students use the rubric throughout the assessment process to see how their work or performance measures up and how they can make it better.

3. Teacher and students use the rubric to discuss the quality of the student's work and performance.

4. Once the work or performance is complete, the teacher provides students with clear feedback about how to make improvements.

The C-List

Purpose: A generative tool that helps the teacher develop good assessment criteria for various tasks. These criteria are then shaped into a rubric.

Procedure: Determining the criteria by which student products and performances will be assessed is one of the most difficult steps in the assessment process. The C-List makes this step simple by providing a comprehensive list of assessment criteria that the teacher selects. There are a number of ways criteria can be selected. They can be:

- selected by the teacher;
- negotiated so that the teacher selects half and the students select half;
- provided as a general list to students, who can select specific criteria themselves;
- used to differentiate assessment so that students with different needs can be assessed according to different criteria.

Once the criteria are selected, the teacher sets up four levels of achievement for each criteria. These levels become the rubric. By using the included form, *Evaluative Words for Creating Rubric Levels,* this step of differentiating between levels of performance is also greatly simplified.

STEPS:

1. The teacher clarifies the requirements of the task.

2. The teacher uses the C-List to select criteria appropriate to the task.

3. The teacher fleshes out the criteria by aligning them with the task. (e.g., What does competence look like specific to this task? What specific content needs to be understood?)

4. Using the form, Evaluative Words for Creating Rubric Levels, the teacher translates steps 1, 2, and 3, into a rubric.

Example: *Using the C-List to Design a Rubric for a Third-Grade Science Task.*

The C-List

Task: <u>To create a zoo exhibit on spiders that is informative and interesting to all audiences</u>

In this activity, I will assess my students' work for: **This dimension will be weighted:**

☐ **Choice:** Does the product reflect careful and sound decision-making processes? _____

☐ **Craftmanship:** Does the student's work reflect care, craftmanship, and high quality? _____

☐ **Completion:** Did the student complete his work in a timely and responsible manner? _____

☑ **Content:** Does the student demonstrate a thorough knowledge of the content at hand? ___1___

☐ **Competence:** Does the work demonstrate competence and knowledge of basic skills? _____

☐ **Character:** Did the student demonstrate a set of positive personal attitudes? _____

☑ **Cooperation:** Can the student contribute to the success of a group? ___1___

☐ **Creativity:** Is the work creative and original? Does it express this student's style? _____

☑ **Communication:** Does the student communicate effectively with diverse audiences? ___1___

☑ **Critical Thinking:** Does the work reflect complex and analytical thought? ___1___

☐ **Complex Problem Solving:** Does the student solve problems thoughtfully? _____

☐ **Others:** _____ _____

☐ _____ _____

The Rubric

Indicators I will stress:

	Spider Facts and Characteristics (Content)	Insight into Environment & Relationships (Critical Thinking)	Audience Interest (Communication)	Cooperation
Master	Exhibit includes all relevant critical characteristics of spiders as a group, and of several specific kinds of spiders; includes information about insects in comparison.	Explanation of environmental relationships (why people and spiders should be friends) is clear, exceptionally insightful, and thoroughly supported.	Exhibit generates and sustains an exceptional level of audience interest, through well-chosen and clearly-communicated facts, stories, and artwork.	The individual student openly and respectfully shared and invited ideas, and was a key player in the success of his or her group.
Journeyman	Exhibit includes four or five critical characteristics of spiders as a group; some information on insects is included.	Explanation of why people and spiders should be friends is clear and thoroughly supported.	Exhibit generates and maintains audience interest through well-chosen facts, stories, and artwork.	The individual student shared and invited ideas, and contributed in some way to the success of the group.
Apprentice	Exhibit includes several spider facts, but some may be inaccurate or irrelevant; little comparative information on insects is included.	Explanation of why people and spiders should be friends is clear, but needs more support; student may not fully understand the connection to environmental issues.	Exhibit generates an acceptable level of interest, but attention may stray; fair choice and communication of facts, stories, and/or artwork.	The individual student actively contributed ideas but was hesitant to invite others to participate; this may have hindered the group's progress.
Novice	Exhibit includes few spider facts, and all are inaccurate; no information on insects.	Explanation of friendship between people and spiders is missing or misconstrued; student failed to understand the purpose or content of the task.	Exhibit fails to generate any interest in the audience; student failed to include relevant or interesting spider trivia.	The student was unable or unwilling to cooperate; seriously affected the work of the group.

The C-List: A Checklist Planner for Assessing Student Work

Task: _____

In this activity, I will assess my students' work for:

This dimension will be weighted:

☐**Choice:** Does the product reflect careful and sound decision-making processes and skills?   _____

☐**Craftmanship:** Does the student's work reflect care, craftmanship, and high quality?   _____

☐**Completion:** Did the student complete his work in a timely and responsible manner?   _____

☐**Content:** Does the student demonstrate a thorough knowledge of the content at hand?   _____

☐**Competence:** Does the work demonstrate competency and a knowledge of basic skills?   _____

☐**Character:** Did the student demonstrate a set of positive personal attitudes?   _____

☐**Cooperation:** Can the student contribute to the success of a group?   _____

☐**Creativity:** Is the work creative and original? Does it express this student's style?   _____

☐**Communication:** Does the student communicate effectively with diverse audiences?   _____

☐**Critical Thinking:** Does the work reflect complex and analytical thought?   _____

☐**Complex Problem Solving:** Does the student solve problems thoughtfully?   _____

☐**Others:** _____   _____

☐   _____   _____

The above dimensions are intended to provide a guide to assessment in style. The choice to assess for each dimension must depend on your classroom, including the curriculum, the task at hand, and especially, the students involved.

Evaluative Words for Creating Rubric Levels

	Master	Journeyman	Apprentice	Novice
☐ Choice	Considerable Thought	Thought	Some Thought	Little or No Thought
☐ Craftsmanship	Outstanding	Good	Fair	Poor
☐ Completion	Complete	Mostly	Somewhat	Incomplete
☐ Content	Deep Understanding	Solid Understanding	Basic Understanding	Little Understanding
☐ Competence	Complete Mastery	Mastery	Partial Mastery	Little Mastery
☐ Character	Exceptional	Evident	Minimal	None
☐ Cooperation	Exceptional	Evident	Minimal	None
☐ Creativity	Highly Original	Mostly Original	Somewhat Original	Unoriginal
☐ Communication	Powerful	Interesting	Standard	Confused
☐ Critical Thinking	Insightful	Evident	Minimal	No Insight
☐ Complex Problem Solving	Disciplined	Thorough	Adequate	Inadequate
☐ Other _____				
☐ Other _____				

Reproducible

Blank Rubric

Task:

Dimension(s) for which I am assess-ing:

Indicators I will stress:

	Master	Journeyman	Apprentice	Novice

Student-Generated Assessment Criteria

Purpose: A set of techniques designed to actively involve students in the assessment process by having them generate the criteria by which their work will be assessed. When students become vested participants in the assessment process, they are more critical of their own work and more likely to strive for excellence.

Procedure: There are three methods for helping students generate quality assessment criteria: the *inductive approach*, the *three-level approach*, and the *high-performance* approach.

In the inductive approach, groups of 3 - 5 students are asked to identify the behaviors of good thinkers or the criteria of specific kinds of work. For example, a history teacher who wants students to conduct a historical research project might ask students to generate a list of the skills and habits of practicing historians, while a journalism teacher might look for students to list the characteristics of a great editorial or feature article. As a class, students generate their ideas and then work to group their ideas into more general categories, which, with refinement become the assessment criteria for a particular task.

The three-level approach is driven by the examination of student work at three levels: high performance, average performance, and low performance. The teacher provides students with sample student work at each of these levels. Working in 3 - 5 member teams, students analyze each sample and identify the criteria that makes each sample representative of its level. Students discuss their criteria as a whole class and together, the students and the teacher use these criteria to develop a rubric for their own work.

The high-performance approach is similar to the three-level approach except that the sample work that students analyze is all representative of high-performance or exemplary work. Student groups analyze the work and record their findings, usually in a three-circle Venn Diagram. (See example below.) In the non-overlapping sections of each circle, students identify the differences between each sample by asking: What makes each unique? In the center, where all three circles overlap, students identify the common attributes of all three samples. The class convenes to discuss their findings and under the teacher's direction, synthesizes the common attributes to create a checklist for assessing their own work.

STEPS:

1. The teacher selects a method for helping students generate criteria (inductive approach, three-level approach, or high-performance approach).

2. Working in groups of 3 - 5 members students either:

- Generate the characteristics of high-quality products or the skills and behaviors of good thinkers (inductive approach)
- Analyze samples of high-performance, average-performance, and low porformance work, and identify and discuss what makes each sample representative of its level (three-level approach)
- Analyze three samples of high performance work, and use a Venn Diagram to identify and discuss the differences and similarities among samples (high-performance approach)

3. The entire class works with the teacher to synthesize ideas and to create a rubric, checklist, or comprehensive set of criteria for assessing student work.

Examples: *All Three Approaches to Generating Student Criteria*

Inductive Approach: A high-school history class about to begin a historical research project generated these skills and behaviors of expert historians:

- Eliminate their own biases
- Write in clear, understandable language
- Are suspicious of "hearsay"
- Are curious
- Look for what history books are missing
- Write in an interesting way
- Want to know why

- Use primary documents
- Use secondary sources
- Interview witnesses and experts (if applicable)
- Check their information
- Take good notes
- Use many sources that show different perspectives

From this list, they created these categories, which became the basis for their class rubric:

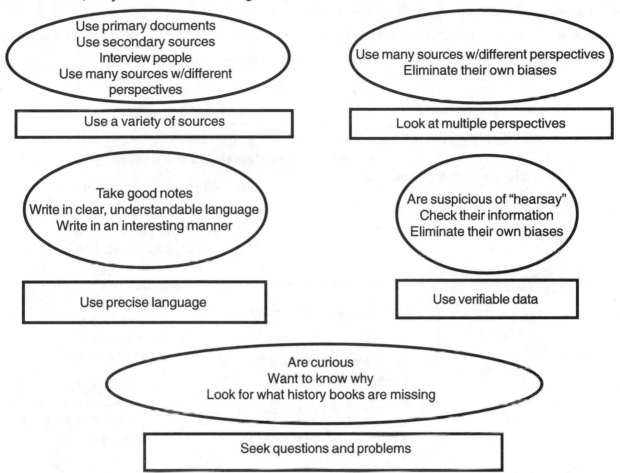

Three-Level Approach: After analyzing high-performance, average-performance, and low-performance examples of persuasive essays, fifth-graders created this organizer with their teacher:

High Performance	Average Performance	Low Performance
Described the author's position at the beginning	Described the position	Never described the position
Used lots of evidence to support the position	Used some evidence to support the position	Can't find evidence
Considered other positions and argued against them	Mentioned other positions	Didn't consider other positions
Has a beginning, middle, and end	A little hard to tell what's the beginning, middle, and end	Writing is confusing
No mistakes in grammar, spelling, or punctuation	A few mistakes	Too many careless mistakes. Needs to proof read better
Used interesting words	Not many interesting words	Lots of short sentences
Used transitions	A few transitions	No transitions

High-Performance Approach: A fourth-grade teacher who wanted her students to write their own fables made a slight variation on the high-performance approach by having students examine three famous fables from different cultures instead of previous students work.

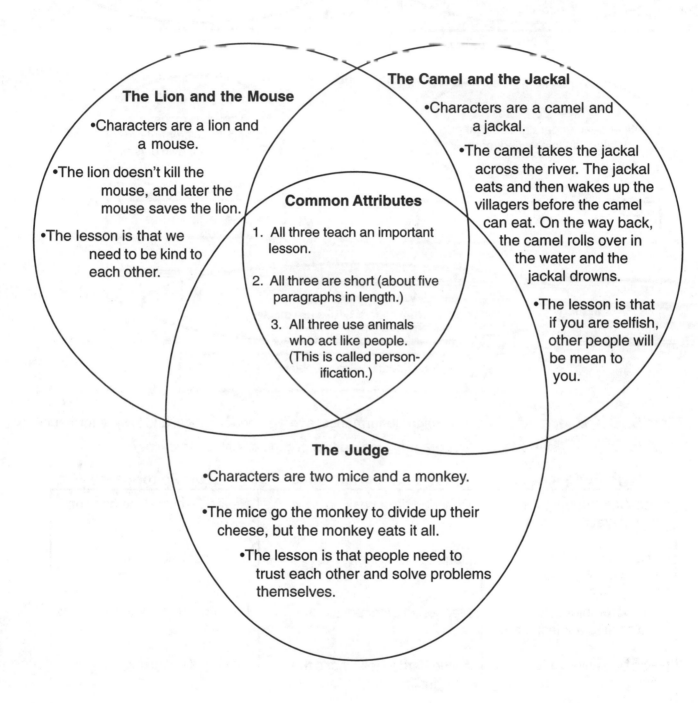

The Lion and the Mouse

•Characters are a lion and a mouse.

•The lion doesn't kill the mouse, and later the mouse saves the lion.

•The lesson is that we need to be kind to each other.

The Camel and the Jackal

•Characters are a camel and a jackal.

•The camel takes the jackal across the river. The jackal eats and then wakes up the villagers before the camel can eat. On the way back, the camel rolls over in the water and the jackal drowns.

•The lesson is that if you are selfish, other people will be mean to you.

Common Attributes

1. All three teach an important lesson.

2. All three are short (about five paragraphs in length.)

3. All three use animals who act like people. (This is called person- ification.)

The Judge

•Characters are two mice and a monkey.

•The mice go the monkey to divide up their cheese, but the monkey eats it all.

•The lesson is that people need to trust each other and solve problems themselves.

Test Feedback

Purpose: A tool for helping students to reflect on their own performance on tests in order to perform better on the next test.

Procedures: Too often, students take tests and then forget about them. The content they had crammed into their brains is set free, and little is retained. Just as damaging, the lessons about test-taking, about how and why a student performs as he does, about the links between instruction, study, and student preparation are never considered, so that the process of cramming and forgetting repeats next time. Test feedback is a metacognitive tool that asks students to reflect on the test, their performance, and how well the classroom instruction and their own study habits prepared them for the test. After the reflection process, a teacher-led discussion helps both the teacher and students to see patterns among students, explore areas of difficulty, and prepare more effectively next time.

Test Feedback also provides the teacher with powerful insight into students' understanding of their own understanding. For instance, when a student thinks he has done well but does poorly, it is often a sign that a student misunderstands a crucial concept that affects the entire test (e.g., order of operations in mathematics). On the other hand, the student who doesn't know how she's done or who thinks she's done poorly but actually does well is often a case of knowing the content but not understanding it. The student has probably been able to plug in the correct information, but without the big picture of a deeper understanding, has very little sense of what she's actually inputting. This kind of information can help the teacher make informed decisions about both test design (e.g., Is it really assessing understanding?) and how to help individual students improve as learners.

STEPS:

1. The teacher provides students with a test-feedback form after they have taken a test.

2. Students reflect on their performance and respond to the questions on the form.

3. The teacher and students discuss the test feedback for the purpose of improving student performance next time.

Example: *Test-Feedback Form for a Test on Cell Structure and Functions*

Circle the face that best describes how you feel about your performance on this test:

Fantastic   **Great**   **Good**   **OK**   **Not Sure**   **I am sick**

Do you think your performance on this test is a good indicator of what you know about the structure of a cell, its parts, and their functions? Why or why not?

Was this test more like a nucleus, cell membrane, cytoplasm, or mitochondria? Explain.

How much time did you spend studying for this test?

How well did the classroom activities prepare you for the test?

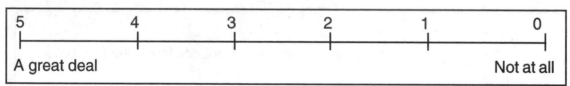

What else would you like to add to demonstrate your knowledge and understanding of this concept?

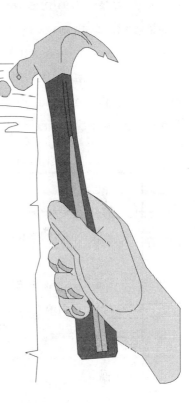

Tools for Promoting Cooperation

Cooperative Structures for Promoting Positive Interdependence

PURPOSE: A set of techniques to promote interdependence and individual accountability in group work.

PROCEDURE. Cooperative Structures are based on the belief that a product produced by a group is usually better than one produced by an individual. The teacher identifies a task that he wants the students to work on cooperatively and then determines a specific structure that is best suited to complete the task. (See examples below.) Each structure creates a need for students to work cooperatively and, at the same time, promotes individual accountability. The teacher must make sure that the students fully understand their roles in the structure. After the work is completed, the teacher grades the students according to the structure that was chosen.

STEPS:

1. The teacher identifies the goals for cooperation and the task to work on cooperatively.

2. The teacher determines which structure is best suited to achieving the goals and completing the task.

3. Students make sure they fully understand their role in each structure.

4. The teacher collects the work and grades appropriately, according to the structure.

Examples: *Six Cooperative Structures*

UNITED WE STAND

In this technique, each group is required to produce one product that compiles each member's best work. For example, each group would develop one set of answers, one chart, one essay, one poem, one illustration, one graph, one diagram, one lab report, etc. Students understand that the group's product should be the result of everyone's efforts and that they will receive a shared grade.

DIFFERENT STROKES

With this technique each group member is expected to provide an individual product after conferring with team members. This technique promotes divergent thinking since students are expected to look for many varied responses to the question. A problem or question is posed and, after group discussion, each student must formulate a unique and correct answer. Students are given credit for every correct group response that is different.

EACH TO HIS OWN

Group members first discuss and combine ideas. Then each member of the group is required to produce an individual product. The group members then check with each other to compare answers. Credit is given for correct and matching responses.

PICK 'EM AT RANDOM

The students work together in a group, making sure that all members of the group have the same answer and can explain how they acquired the answer. The teacher then randomly calls on one student to represent the group and share the group's answer. A shared grade is given to each group member.

SIGN OFF

This technique ensures student cooperation and accountability within the group structure. Each group member must sign all work that is submitted, but all members must agree that each student has done appropriate work before the signature is allowed. This technique promotes high levels of cooperation because the signature guarantees that all students have worked on the question, that they understand the answer, and that they can explain and defend the group's position if asked to do so.

DIVIDED RESOURCES

This technique limits resources given to each group member so that the members of the group must share materials and work cooperatively. The teacher may give each member of the group different documents or clues needed to solve a mystery or a puzzle. The teacher might provide each group with one worksheet containing the questions, one map from which to work, one copy of directions, one pen that must be shared, etc. Each method ensures that students work together.

Learning Partners

Purpose: A technique used to involve everyone in a collaborative activity, especially when there is insufficient time to establish small discussion groups or to complete a cooperative learning activity.

Procedure: Learning Partners is an efficient and effective way to promote active learning. A pair is a good configuration for developing supportive relationships and for working on complex tasks. It is difficult to get left out of a pair; it is also difficult to hide in one. With this technique the teacher determines the type of task students will complete (e.g., read and discuss a document), then establishes pairs and the amount of time students will have to work on the task. During the work the teacher should walk around the room, monitoring student performance and judging how much time students will need to complete the task. Students should not be stopped abruptly from working. The teacher will announce to the students that they have a minute to complete their task and that they should look up as they finish. After the partners have completed their task, the teacher should collect student responses and then ask students to reflect upon their work and how they worked together to complete the task.

STEPS:

1. The teacher determines the task.

2. The teacher establishes partnerships and time to complete the task.

3. The teacher monitors student work and brings students to a gradual stop.

4. The teacher collects responses and leads discussion.

5. Students reflect upon the task and partnerships.

Examples: *Eleven Ideas for Learning Partners*

1. Interview another student concerning reactions to an assigned reading or lecture.

2. Critique or edit each other's written work.

3. Summarize a lesson or class discussion.

4. Read and review. Both read a page together, stop, and then one partner asks questions while the other closes the book. Reverse roles.

5. Develop questions together to ask the teacher.

6. Test each other on materials presented in class.

7. Respond to questions posed by the teacher.

8. Compare notes taken in class.

9. Analyze a case study.

10. Conduct an experiment.

11 Complete an exercise or problem set together.

Team-O-Graph

Purpose: A tool that helps students assess their own collaborative skills and the overall functioning of their team.

Procedure: Team-O-Graph is a simple tool for students to use after working in a group. Once group work has been completed, students fill out the Team-O-Graph form to assess their own contributions, those of their team members, and the working of the entire group. Because the form is confidential, students are more likely to be honest in their appraisal of the team. Additionally, the use of the Team-O-Graph greatly reduces the possibility of students freeloading off of other group members, since all group members' contributions will be confidentially reported.

STEPS:

1. After group work, the teacher distributes a Team-O-Graph form to all students.

2. Students fill out the Team-O-Graph form individually and confidentially.

3. The teacher reviews the Team-O-Graph forms to develop a realistic assessment of each group's functioning and individual's contributions.

(c) 2001, The Thoughtful Education Press
(800) 962-4432

A Team-O-Graph Form For Students

A Confidential Evaluation of My Team

Name: _____

The Effort Graph		Horribly				Perfectly
		1	2	3	4	5
	How well did my team work together?					
		1	2	3	4	5
	How well did each team member work? _____ _____ _____ _____	_____ _____ _____ _____				

Comments on the Team: _____

_____

_____

_____

My greatest challenges during this activity: _____

_____

_____

_____

My greatest contributions during this activity: _____

_____

_____

_____

Tools for Energizing Learning

Energizers

Purpose: Tools used primarily to liven up, energize, activate, and stimulate the minds and bodies of learners. Recent brain research tells us that physical stimulation boosts mental activity, that learning done with the mind and body is generally more effective than learning done with the mind only; and that the engagement of emotions increases the impact and recall of the learning experience.

Procedures/Variations:

Add-Ons

One person is invited to come up to the front of the room and act out or present something that he has learned from the class. Another comes up and joins the impromptu living sculpture. Others come up, one at a time, to add to the giant scenario that represents what the class has learned.

Around the World

All the students are asked to stand up at the back of the room. A question is asked either by the teacher or a student. The students write their answers on paper. If the answer is correct, they can take a step forward. Each question is worth a certain number of steps depending upon its degree of difficulty. This technique is great for spatial and kinesthetic learners.

Ball Toss

Five to seven students stand in a circle ten feet apart. One ball or a bean bag is provided. The student with the ball or beanbag is responsible for responding, then tossing it to another student, who must continue. Content can be Q and A, items in a category, word association, continuation of a story, etc.

Barnyard

This tool provides an energizing way to form groups. Assign numbers to students according to the number of groups you want (with eight groups, everyone gets a number from 1-8). Assign a noisy animal to each number: all ones are dogs, all twos are cats, all threes are goats, all fours are horses, all fives are sheep, all sixes are chickens, all sevens are ducks, and all eights are mules. Then have all the students stand up and mix, making the appropriate noise of their animal and trying to find the other members of their group. To add to the fun and difficulty, have students close their eyes and try to find the members of their group.

Birthday Lines

Invite students to stand up. Ask them to get into single file, in order of their birthdays from January 1 to December 31. To add to the fun, divide the class in two and have students compete to see which half is the fastest, or have them line up without speaking. Have students discuss what they learned from this process about problem-solving, teamwork, and communication.

Chalk Talk

Put a question on the board. Then invite students to come to the board one at a time to respond. Each student can come up to the board and respond to the question, the prompt, or the previous student's response.

Pictionary

Divide the class into teams. Select several concepts that you have taught and put each one on a card. Invite a member of a team to come to the board and draw a picture without words that represents the idea. The other members of the team have three (3) minutes to figure out the idea being communicated to them. This is an excellent activity to stimulate spatial/visual intelligence.

Commercial Breaks

This tool is a great technique to review information. Divide the class into teams. Each team is assigned a topic, or teams choose their own. Each team is responsible for developing an impromptu television commercial. The point of the commercial is to review the content. This can also be done with partners or by individuals.

Expert Interviews

Half the students become experts in the topic you are teaching and half are interviewers. The interviewers have two minutes to get the story. The roles are then reversed.

Human Knot

The class is divided into six eight-person teams. Each team stands in a circle. Each member grabs the hand of a team member next to him and the hand of someone in the circle not next to him. Check that everyone is connected. One person squeezes the hand of the person next to him; that person squeezes the other hand of the next person and so on until the "squeeze" returns to the person who started it. The students are then asked to untangle themselves so that they are all facing the same way in the circle holding hands. The one important rule is that the group can not break hands at any time.

Inquiry

The teacher selects specific terms or names of people that she wants the students to remember and writes each one on a card. Each student is given a card and asked to tape it on the back of another student. One card is given to each student. The students then stand up and walk around the room, looking at the backs of all the other students. Students stop and ask other students yes or no questions to collect information about the card they are wearing before they guess the card. When they think they know the concept, they make a guess. If they are correct, they wear the card in front. When all students have guessed their terms, the teacher has the students form groups of terms that go together and has each group explain why its members go together.

One Interesting Fact

Students are handed a card and asked to write something about themselves that no one knows and that they are comfortable sharing. After the card is written, each student stands up. When all the cards are complete, the teacher distributes the cards back to different students. The students then have to walk around the room, trying to find the person who has their card. Calling out is not permitted, and students can ask only one person at a time. When students have been found and have found the person they were looking for, they return to their seat.

Square Dance

The students form two circles, one inside the other, with students in each circle facing each other. A command is given to the members of one or both circles. The teacher may say, "Inside circle walk three steps to the right; outside circle, two steps to the left." Participants stop in front of their new partner and are asked a question to consider. They discuss their responses. The question can be content oriented (e.g., Which character in the book is most like you and why?) or personally oriented, (e.g., If you found $25.00 what would you do with the money?).

Scrunches

Have the students "scrunch" their toes, then their ankles, and continue up the torso to the top of their heads until their whole body is scrunched tightly. Then have them release the scrunch slowly from the top of their head to their toes. This increases the blood flow through the body and brings oxygen to the cells which, in turn, enhances students' ability to think.

Selected Bibliography

Benevento, E. S. (1997). *The giver: A thinker's guide to literature.* Woodbridge, NJ: The Thoughtful Education Press.

Brooks, J. G., & Brooks, M. G. (1993). *In search of understanding: The case for constructivist classrooms.* Alexandria, VA: Association for Supervision and Curriculum Development.

Brownlie, F., & Close, S. (1992). *Beyond chalk and talk: Collaborative strategies for middle and high school years.* Markham, Ontario: Pembroke Publishers, Ltd.

Brownlie, F., & Silver, H. F. (1995). *Mind's eye.* Paper presented at the seminar "Responding Thoughtfully to the Challenge of Diversity," Delta School District Conference Center, Delta, British Columbia, Canada.

Caine, G., & Caine, R. N. (Eds.). (1994). *Making connections: Teaching and the human brain.* Menlo Park, CA: Addison-Wesley.

Davis, H. B., & Dudley, A. H. (1994). *Definition: The assessment library.* Woodbridge, NJ: The Thoughtful Education Press.

Herber, H. (1970). *Teaching reading in the content areas.* Englewood Cliffs, NJ: Prentice Hall.

Morris, S., & McCarthy, B. (1999). *4MAT in action.* Wauconda, IL: About Learning, Inc.

Murnane, R. J., & Levy, F. (1996). *Teaching the new basic skills: Principles for educating children to thrive in a changing economy.* New York, NY: The Free Press.

Ogle, D. (1986). K-W-L: A teaching model that develops active reading of the expository text. *The Reading Teacher*, 39, 564-570.

Pauk, W. (1974). *How to study in college.* Boston, MA: Houghton Mifflin.

Reich, R. B. (1992). *The work of nations.* New York, NY: Vintage Books.

Resnick, L. B. (1987). The 1987 presidential address: Learning in school and out. *Educational Researcher*, 16 (9).

Silver, H. F., & Hanson, J. R. (1998). *Learning styles and strategies* (3rd ed.). Woodbridge, NJ: The Thoughtful Education Press.

Silver, H. F., & Strong, R.W. (1998). *Write to learn.* Woodbridge, NJ: The Thoughtful Education Press.

Sparks, J. E. (1982). *Write for power.* Los Angeles, CA: Communication Associates.

Strong, R. W., Hanson, J. R., & Silver, H. F. (1995). *Questioning styles and strategies* (2nd ed.). Woodbridge, NJ: The Thoughtful Education Press.